THE PIONEER SPIRIT

THE PIONEER SPIRIT

Mal Fletcher

Authentic

Copyright © 2001, 2005 Mal Fletcher

09 08 07 06 05   7 6 5 4 3 2 1
First published in English by Next Wave International™
155 Regents Park Road, London, NW1 8BB.

This edition published by Authentic Media,
9 Holdom Avenue, Bletchley, Milton Keynes, MK1 1QR and
P.O. Box 1047, Waynesboro, GA 30830-2047, USA.

The right of Mal Fletcher to be identified as the author of this
work has been asserted by him in accordance with the
Copyright, Designs and Patents Act 1988.
All rights reserved.

No part of this publication may be reproduced or transmitted in
any form or by any means, electronic or mechanical, including
photocopy, recording or any information storage and retrieval
system, without permission in writing from the publisher.

British Library Cataloguing in Publication Data
A catalogue record for this book is available from the British Library

1-86024-519-6

Unless otherwise indicated, all Scripture quotations are from the
HOLY BIBLE, NEW INTERNATIONAL VERSION.
Copyright 1973, 1978, 1984 by International Bible Society.
Used by permission of Hodder & Stoughton, a member of
Hodder Headline Ltd. All rights reserved.

Cover design by David Lund
Print Management by Adare Carwin
Printed and Bound in Denmark by Nørhaven Paperback

www.malfletcher.com

What major Christian leaders say about Mal Fletcher

'Mal Fletcher is a man with a mission. I love his zeal, his enthusiasm and his deep commitment to reach hurting humanity with the Good News of the Gospel. Mal is truly a man born for such a time as this.'
Dr Jerry Savelle, President, JSMI, USA

'There are some who merely watch things happen, as the saying goes, and some who make things happen: the observers and the activists. But every now and then you come across a man with the unique ability to do both; he who both sees with a prophet's eye what is going on in the world and has the gifting to affect it with power. Mal Fletcher is one of these men. He is a thinker, an artist, and above all a man who loves God and loves people.'
Winkie Pratney, Author & Evangelist

'Today, we are seeing the emergence of powerful new ideas that are permeating our society. The combination of new ideas and advanced technology sometimes makes the church seem stale, stuffy and irrelevant. One man I know who is addressing the issues, and has insight into what the church needs to become, is my friend Mal Fletcher. He has been a special blessing to me in this area, giving new insight to both me and the body of Christ in South Africa.'
Pastor Ray McCauley, Senior Pastor, Rhema Church, South Africa

'Mal has committed his life to making God famous, and his passion for this purpose has influenced thousands of young adults all over the earth to go out and do the same. If you long to make an impact for Jesus in the twenty-first century, then this book is for you!'
Pastor Brian Houston, Senior Pastor, Hillsong Church, Australia

'If you're called to be a pioneer but have become a settler, this book is for you. It's written to bring you back to the lip of the wave, the coalface, the frontier. Behind the book is a man who's living is now – pioneering the way for a new generation of Luthers, Livingstones, Mandelas and Tyndales. It could be your turn to take the mantle. This book's a "must-read".'
Dave Gilpin, Senior Minister, Hope City Church, Sheffield, UK

'Today, there are many people trying to make themselves famous, seeking fame and fortune. Mal Fletcher, however, has proven himself a faithful man of God whose life truly seeks to make GOD famous. He has a powerful anointing to communicate the gospel and his life inspires many, including Mark and me, as he follows the call of God to change the face of Europe. Not only will this book bless and inspire you; it will challenge you to do every thing you can to make God famous today!'

Darlene Zschech, Hillsong Music, Australia

'Mal Fletcher is a key communicator in today's culture. He carries the unique blend of creative and provocative thought with a solid and biblical foundation. He is not just a man of words but also a man of action. The fruit of his ministry can be seen right across Europe.'

Pastor Stuart Bell, Leader, Ground Level
Network of Churches, UK

'Mal Fletcher has the unique ability to discern the needs in today's international Western culture and to articulate, in a powerful, relevant way, the biblical solutions to those needs. He is being used by God to help shape the emerging leaders in today's church, especially throughout Western Europe. Mal is a man with a message that needs to be heard.'

Pastor Bayless Conley, Senior Pastor,
Cottonwood Christian Centre, USA

'Mal Fletcher is an Aussie legend. Rarely has someone left our shores with so little and accomplished so much. I totally endorse Mal. I believe he is an end-time leader with an amazing anointing on his life. His integrity and his passion so inspire me. Mal's my hero!'

Pastor Jack Hanes, President, First Priority
(AOG World Missions), Australia

'As a friend and colleague of Mal Fletcher, I have always found his written works to be both stimulating and faith building. I consider reading a Mal Fletcher book a must. It will always leave you feeling equipped and ready for the leadership challenge.'

Pastor Danny Guglielmucci, Senior Pastor,
Southside Christian Church, Australia

Contents

1.	Pioneer World Changers	1
2.	Pioneer Passion	14
3.	Designing the Future	36
4.	Re-digging the Wells	56
5.	You Are That Road Runner!	73
6.	Pioneer Alliances	91
7.	Pioneering: What a Ride	110
8.	Jesus On the Airwaves	127
9.	Beyond Church-on-TV	144
	About the Author	167

Special Thanks

As you'll see in this book, I believe strongly in the benefits of networks, alliances and covenants. Pioneer leaders can't function without them. I just want to thank some people whose friendship and like-minded faith has made this project possible.

Special thanks to:

Davina, my wife and partner in faith. Thanks for standing with me in everything. Pioneer leadership is not an easy path, but you have always been so totally willing to walk it with me.

Deanna, Grant and Jade, my great children who are now rising up for God in their own right. Keep the faith and pioneer new things for a new generation! Each of you is destined for great things.

Our Core Alliance Partners. Pioneers need Antioch churches. Without your support, we couldn't keep seeing results across Europe and beyond.

Our Next Wave International team, past and present. Thanks for your risk-taking faith!

Those who helped to produce this book – in particular Malcolm Down, the team at Authentic Media (UK), Craig Moulton and Word Australia. Also to Mike Staires, Ben Ferrell and Chris Busch and Team BMC in Tulsa.

To all my pioneer-leader friends around the world, in church, media and other spheres of influence. You inspire me, as you do so many thousands of others. In everything you do, you demonstrate the principles outlined in this book. You embody the pioneer spirit. Keep making God famous!

Mal Fletcher
June 2004

1

Pioneer World Changers

It is August 28, 1963. A man of vision stands on the steps of the Lincoln Memorial in Washington DC. He looks out over a vast crowd and prepares to address them. Here on this day, at this hour, he will call his nation to account. He will remind America of the promise put forth at its founding.

'I still have a dream,' he declares. 'It is a dream deeply rooted in the American dream.

'I have a dream that one day this nation will rise up and live out the true meaning of its creed: "We hold these truths to be self-evident: that all men are created equal."

'I have a dream that one day on the red hills of Georgia the sons of former slaves and the sons of former slave-owners will be able to sit down together at a table of brotherhood.

'I have a dream that one day even the state of Mississippi, a desert state, sweltering with the heat of injustice and oppression, will be transformed into an oasis of freedom and justice.

'I have a dream that my four children will one day live in a nation where they will not be judged by the colour of their skin but by the content of their character.

'I have a dream today.'

The Pioneer Spirit

The forward progress of every great human endeavour has come about through the work of pioneers. Whatever the venture, in whatever field, momentous achievements have always been the result of the pioneer spirit.

In the domain of race relations, we think of Dr Martin Luther King, a true pathfinder. Our hearts stir within us whenever we hear those historic words 'I have a dream.'

In the sphere of education – and care of the disabled – we celebrate Helen Keller, another innovator. In the realm of social action, we remember with fondness the groundbreaking compassion of Mother Teresa. In the arena of political reform, we gratefully acknowledge the contribution of Nelson Mandela. Adventure sports bring to mind the courageous exploits of Sir Edmund Hilary and space exploration owes an enormous debt to Neil Armstrong. The list goes on and on. Pioneers light the spark of every truly momentous undertaking.

In the Christian church, we have much to celebrate. Through the centuries, our faith has inspired some of the world's most influential pioneers.

Our heritage in the pioneer spirit began with the great evangelist Paul. This man almost single-handedly opened up the ancient Gentile world to the message about Jesus. Before his trailblazing work, the Christian message had been almost exclusively the property of Jewish people or converts to Judaism. Jesus' own apostles had, for the most part, worked among the Jews.

Striking out against the trend, Paul planted churches among Jews *and* Gentiles, first in Asia Minor and the Balkans and then in Macedonia and into Western Europe. 'Paul is the intellectual forbear of anyone who was brought up within the framework of ... Europe,' writes media commentator, Edward Stourton. 'He is one of a handful of towering figures who formed our way of thinking and when you read his letters you are going back to your roots.'[1]

Pioneer World Changers 3

Paul's influence can still be felt today. In his letter to the Christians in Rome, he told us what motivated him for ministry and mission:

I have trailblazed a preaching of the Message of Jesus all the way from Jerusalem far into northwestern Greece. This has all been pioneer work, bringing the Message only into those places where Jesus was not yet known and worshipped. My text has been, 'Those who were never told of him – they'll see him! Those who've never heard of him – they'll get the message.' (Romans 15:19–21, The Message)

Paul was driven forward by the passion of an innovator, a pioneer. Through the centuries that followed, the same spirit drove many other Christians who altered the course of history.

John Wesley saved England from revolution, sparing it the bloodshed seen in France. George Müller initiated Europe's first orphan houses, rescuing thousands of children from a miserable death on Dickensian streets. William Wilberforce worked for over a generation to overthrow the practice of slavery in the British Isles. His legacy was a moral movement that ended this vile trade in the United States as well.

Nikolaus Ludwig Zinzendorf, an East German nobleman, led a group of religious exiles from Moravia who founded the Christian community of Herrnhut on his estate. From their number sprang a missions movement that still touches the world today.

David Livingstone opened up the heart of Africa to civilization and education. He made such an indelible impact on his generation that his funeral drew more people to the streets of London than that of any other person outside the royal family. William and Catherine

The Pioneer Spirit

Booth defied the religious convention of their time to bring relief to millions who were suffering in urban poverty and shame. In so doing, they gave the world the Salvation Army.

'A saint,' wrote G. K. Chesterton, 'is one who exaggerates what the world neglects.' For many centuries, the church produced some of most radical, transformative pioneers the world has ever seen. True Christian saints helped to shape history for the good.

All that, however, began to change around one hundred and fifty to two hundred years ago. It began with Charles Darwin announcing that human beings are just amoebae that decided to climb from the primordial slime. We are nothing more than croutons that evolved in nature's prehistoric soup.

In Darwin's scheme of things, human beings were no longer considered the product of divine choice and design; they were simply the outcome of random evolutionary processes. In the space of just one generation, we went from being children of God to children of algae!

Soon, other European thinkers were taking Darwin's naturalistic ideas in the field of biology and applying them to all areas of human experience. In Germany, Frederick Nietzsche proclaimed that 'God is dead and we have killed him.' In France, the philosopher Rousseau advocated that, since God was no longer relevant, the state should take over his role. Karl Marx followed much the same line. His teachings on politics and economics gave rise to communism, the saddest social experiment in human history.

In all this time, people thought that by abandoning God they would be free to release the fullness of human potential. They discovered instead that when we reject God, we plumb human nature's darkest depths. Writing to the early Christians in Rome, Paul told us that

Pioneer World Changers

whenever people have forgotten God they have 'trivialized themselves into silliness and confusion so that there was neither sense nor direction left in their lives.'[2]

Meanwhile, after hundreds of years of setting the course of history through pioneer conquest, the church allowed its role to change. Overwhelmed by a flood of utopian, naturalistic philosophies, the church found itself becoming reactive rather than proactive. Constantly on the back foot, it found itself responding to change rather than initiating it. Consequently, many Christians and churches adopted a mentality that was more about maintenance and management than breaking new ground.

New Pioneers

The word had gone around the small Indian village: a rich merchant had come to town and was offering high prices for local land.

Excited, landowners and householders rushed to meet the man with the money. They found him willing to pay them far more than their properties were actually worth. His quest, it seemed, was to fulfil a lifelong dream. He wanted to be able to say, 'I own an entire village.'

Because they'd never seen so much money in their lives, the humble villagers gladly took the cash and waved goodbye to their homes. Everyone sold out to the rich merchant – everyone, that is, except one stubborn old man. He defiantly resisted all offers, no matter how exorbitant.

Thereafter, the rich man would often come to town to show his friends the town he owned. Without fail, the old man would stand in his doorway and shout across the street: 'If he tells you he owns it all, don't believe it! I still own *this* piece!'

6　　　*The Pioneer Spirit*

The church in much of the Western world is like that old man. It obstinately struggles to hold on to what little influence it still has, rather than pushing forward to take new ground.

Since the Enlightenment, the Western church has often been more about establishing a subculture that mirrors the status quo than raising up a prophetic alternative to challenge it.

In our time, though, God is raising up a new pioneer generation. A new kind of leadership is emerging in the churches of Western nations – often taking its lead from churches in the East and the developing world. It is not celebrated in the glossy magazines of popular culture, but this new breed of leaders is nevertheless growing in influence. They are determined to recapture the adventurous, world-challenging passion of first-century Christianity. They have set their face to take up the challenge others have found too costly: to walk according to their sovereign calling instead of their social conditioning.

There are many ways to describe what it means to be a pioneer. One definition says that a pioneer is someone who is the first to do something or go somewhere. Another states that pioneers blaze new trails. I think, though, that the most succinct definition says this: 'Pioneers create breakthroughs for themselves and for other people.'

It's right that we celebrate certain people as pioneers of special courage, yet we all need the pioneer spirit in the face of life's many challenges. Every day, we face situations in which we need breakthroughs, for ourselves and for people around us.

Reading this book right now, you will see areas of your own life where you want and need to blaze new trails of possibility and opportunity. Perhaps you are a parent, like me, who wants to forge a better life for yourself and for your children. You may be a businessman or woman

Pioneer World Changers 7

who dreams of creating wealth and opportunities for yourself and your employees. Perhaps you're a student and you want to invest your gifts to create a better future for yourself and for others. Or you may be a pastor or church department leader and you long to see people growing in maturity and impacting their world.

Whatever our particular situation in life, none of us can really afford to have more of the same – we each need to blaze new trails. We need less of the management mentality and more pathfinder passion! The truly *great* news is that God wants to help each of us to achieve those groundbreaking goals.

God, the Pioneer

The God revealed in the Bible is, by nature, a pioneer. That much is clear from the very first stanza of the Bible. As the great drama of revelation begins, the curtain opens to reveal a God who is creating, innovating, pioneering.

You only have to look at the intricate complexity of the human body to see how ingenious God is. The great inventor Isaac Newton had this to say: 'In the absence of any other proof, the [human] thumb alone would convince me of God's existence.' With its incredible range of motion, the thumb, says Howard Hendricks, 'mirrors an inventive brilliance of astounding proportions.'[3]

Consider, too, the human eye. There are tiny muscles within your eye that move it between thirty and seventy times per minute. These movements are so small that you don't notice them. In size, every movement is just one-seventieth the thickness of a piece of paper! Yet, without these constant, minute adjustments, your eyes would never be able to focus.

8 *The Pioneer Spirit*

Theologians like to say that God created *ex nihilo* – out of nothing. Until fairly recently, artists never used the word 'creative' to describe themselves or their work. They felt that this would be presumptuous, as the only truly original creator is God. When we do something creative, we're only reshaping what is already before us.

C. S. Lewis writes this: '"Creation" as applied to human authorship seems to me to be an entirely misleading term. We rearrange elements [God] has provided. There is not a vestige of real creativity *de novo* in us. Try to imagine a new primary colour, a third sex, a further dimension, or even a monster that does not consist of bits of existing animals stuck together. Nothing happens. And that surely is why our works . . . never mean to others quite what we intended: because we are re-combining elements made by Him and already containing His meanings.'[4]

Put simply: for all our inventiveness, we still cannot create something from nothing as God did 'in the beginning'.

God's pioneer activity is not restricted to the first chapter of Genesis. Throughout the Bible, we repeatedly find God doing things for the first time, in ways that take people by surprise. The movie *The Matrix* showed us the exciting possibilities of inter-dimensional travel. Yet, this is no new thing. Genesis tells us that, '[The prophet] Enoch . . . was no more, because God took him away.'[5] Enoch simply vanished from the scene of time, transported to a higher dimension. God is the initiator; movie producers simply follow his lead!

When most of us think of molecular transportation, *Star Trek* movies and TV shows come to mind ('beam me up Scotty'). But God was doing this kind of thing long before the USS Enterprise ever left port! Acts says, 'The Spirit of the Lord suddenly took Philip away . . . [and he] appeared at Azotus.'[6] Long, long ago, in a galaxy *not* so

Pioneer World Changers

far away, the Christian evangelist Philip actually *experienced* molecular displacement. Again, God the innovator was at work.

Not long ago, *Time* magazine celebrated the mapping of the human genome. The writers marvelled at the fact that scientists are able to identify individual genes and their particular coding. This is certainly a major achievement. Read your New Testament, though, and you find that God has already 'been there, done that'. Matthew's gospel says that even the hairs on our heads are numbered.[7]

Jesus, the Inventor of Our Faith

Jesus Christ was a pioneer – the greatest of them all. Hendricks says, 'Nowhere is the unanticipated – a hallmark of creativity – more obvious than in the life and ministry of our Lord.'[8]

Think about it: how many great innovations have resulted from Jesus' influence in history? Dr Martin Luther King had a dream *because* he was a follower of Christ. Mother Teresa gave dignity to the poor and leprous *because* she was devoted to Christ. Ghandi gave us his philosophy of passive resistance *because* he was influenced by the teachings of Christ.

Banished to the rock of St Helena, Napoleon Bonaparte, the conqueror of civilized Europe, had time to reflect on what he'd accomplished. Deep in thought, he called a nobleman to his side and asked him, 'Can you tell me who Jesus Christ was?' The nobleman wouldn't answer.

'Well then,' said Napoleon, 'I will tell you.

'Alexander, Caesar, Charlemagne and I myself have founded great empires; but upon what did these creations of our genius depend? Upon force. Jesus alone

10   *The Pioneer Spirit*

founded His empire upon love, and to this very day millions will die for Him . . .

'I think I understand something of human nature; and I tell you, all these were men, and I am a man: none else is like Him; Jesus Christ was more than man . . . I have inspired multitudes with such an enthusiastic devotion that they would have died for me . . . but to do this it was necessary that I should be visibly present with the electric influence of my looks, my words, of my voice . . .

'Christ alone has succeeded in so raising the mind of man toward the unseen, that it becomes insensible to the barriers of time and space.

'Across a chasm of eighteen hundred years, Jesus Christ makes a demand which is beyond all others difficult to satisfy . . . He asks for the human heart; He will have it entirely to Himself. He demands it unconditionally; and forthwith His demand is granted.

'Wonderful! In defiance of time and space, the soul of man, with all its powers and faculties, becomes an annexation to the empire of Christ. All who sincerely believe in Him, experience that remarkable, supernatural love toward Him. [This is what leads me to believe] in the Divinity of Jesus Christ.'[9]

H. G. Wells expressed something similar when he looked back at the life and times of Jesus. 'More than 1,900 years later,' he wrote, 'a historian like me who doesn't even call himself a Christian, finds the picture [of history] centring irresistibly around the life and character of this most significant man . . . The historian's test of an individual's greatness is, "What did he leave to grow?" Did he start men to thinking along fresh lines with a vigour that persisted after him? By this test, Jesus stands first.'[10]

Despite early opposition that saw many of its members

Pioneer World Changers

nailed to crosses or burned alive for their faith, the church has survived to the present day. Despite countless attempts to destroy the holy book on which it feeds, the church's faith has grown stronger with every attack. Despite the efforts of kings and warriors to bring it under human control, the kingdom that Jesus started refuses to be held back or reigned in. It is a dominion born in human hearts and it outlasts all other kingdoms.

Today, many of us wear crosses as jewellery around our necks and in our ears. For us, the cross is a symbol of compassion, affection, mercy and kindness. When Jesus encountered a cross, however, it was anything but a symbol of love.

The Roman cross was one of most cruel instruments of torture and death ever devised by the human mind. You could say that it was the gas chamber of the ancient world, except that, while it was just as agonizing, it took longer to finish you off. People would hang on crosses for days, gasping for breath while every nerve and sinew cried out in excruciating agony. Suspended and exposed to the elements, they would pray for death to come and end their anguish.

Yet, Jesus took this abominable instrument of cruelty and turned it into the world's most recognized icon of love. He transmuted a notorious machine of horror into a sign of hope. Jesus transformed the cross into God's advertising symbol. In so doing, he blazed a new trail and created breakthroughs for others. He opened up a path of favour with God. He became, says Romans 8:29, the 'firstborn among many brothers'.

God the Father is a pioneer, as is the Son. So, too, is the Holy Spirit. His arrival saw the birth of the church in supernatural power. The Christian church was not instituted by human design or activity. The church was born out of the supernatural working of the Holy Spirit.

12 *The Pioneer Spirit*

So it is today. The church is not built on its leaders, its programmes, its structure or its style of presentation. The church is established upon the nature and work of the Holy Spirit who reveals Jesus and exalts the Father. The church grows in new areas, and is regenerated in old ones, as the Holy Spirit brings people to rebirth and empowers them for witness.

Whatever your situation and status in life, the Holy Spirit wants to equip *you* to cut a new path, to create breakthroughs for yourself and others. This book is not about how to *create* the pioneer spirit. If you are a Christian, the Spirit of Christ energizes your life and the zeal of the pioneer already lives in you. This book is about how you can *release* that creative power so that you can cut a new path for your future, in line with God's promise.

President George W. Bush, responding to the painful events of September 11, 2001, called on his nation to rise up once again to fight for the cause of freedom. 'The cause of our fathers,' he said, 'has now become the calling of our time.'

This book carries a similar call to generations within the Christian church. It is time for us to put off maintenance mentality and to release the spirit of innovation and risk-taking action. The flame that burned so fiercely in the souls of our fathers must inspire *our* hearts to challenge the status quo and point the way to something better.

It is time for us to make God famous, by releasing the pioneer spirit.

1. Edward Stourton, *A 2000 Year Journey in the Telegraph Weekend*, Saturday, March 2, 2002
2. Romans 1:21, *The Message*

Pioneer World Changers

3. Howard Hendricks, *Color Outside The Lines* (Word Publishing, 1998), p. 30
4. Quoted by Howard Hendricks, ibid., p. 20
5. Genesis 5:24
6. Acts 8:39–40
7. Matthew 10:30
8. Hendricks, Op. Cit., p. 12
9. Quoted by Ravi Zacharias, *Jesus Among Other Gods* (Word Publishing, 2000), pp. 149–150
10. Quoted by Philip Yancey, *The Jesus I Never Knew* (Zondervan Publishing House, 1995), p. 17

2

Pioneer Passion

It is just a few hours after the horror of September 11, 2001.

America – indeed, the world – has never experienced anything like it. Young zealots from the other side of the globe, motivated by a potent mixture of religious fervour and hate, have crashed four airliners filled with people. Two of those planes have reduced the sky-scraping towers of the World Trade Centre to rubble.

Standing amid the devastation on the dust covered streets of New York, a leading TV journalist stoops to pick up a piece of paper, one of the many business documents fluttering in the murky air. It is a simple letter drafted on corporate letterhead.

'Yesterday,' she says, 'this piece of paper was probably the most important thing in the world to somebody. Today, it is totally meaningless.'

September 11, 2001 changed many things. It impacted the way we travel, it altered the way we look at high-rise buildings and, for a while, it even changed the way some of us opened our mail.

It also shook our faith in the institutions of society that are said to protect us – or, at least the ones we hadn't

Pioneer Passion

already come to doubt. In his classic book, *SoulTsunami*, Leonard Sweet writes that in a post-modern world we have access to all the information we could ever need, and yet, 'Everything is breaking up and up for grabs. Most of our institutions are adrift, washed up at sea, or abandoned ashore, beached by the tide of history, turning to "dust and crashes".'[1] If that was true before the WTC towers came down, it is certainly true now.

As the French proverb has it, the more things change, the more they stay the same. For all our symbols of wealth and power, we are still, at root, looking for a deeper kind of security – a security that comes through family and community. When that also breaks down, or comes under threat, we need something deeper still; we need verities that transcend time or culture, or even human reason.

September 11, 2001 reminded us of this. This date has become a defining moment for a nation and for the world. Social commentators now talk in terms of 'pre-9/11' and 'post-9/11'.

If the horrific events of that tragic day show us nothing else, they certainly reveal the power of passion. The whole thing began with an unleashing of passion for evil; a commitment to a cause that led young men to commit mass murder and suicide. This kind of ardour is incomprehensible to most of us.

The ancient wisdom of the biblical Proverbs tells us:

It is not good to have zeal without knowledge, nor to be hasty and miss the way. A man's own folly ruins his life, yet his heart rages against the LORD. (Proverbs 19:2–3)

The anger shown by the perpetrators of these horrors was not just directed at America, or even Western civilisation. It was aimed at God himself. No matter how

16 *The Pioneer Spirit*

righteous men may say is their cause, no man can so cruelly snuff out human life – which God calls sacred – and truly claim to be acting in concert with God. September 11 was a day of sinful anger gone mad.

Yet, there was also a remarkable passion for good revealed on that day. Who can forget, for example, the totally admirable courage of emergency workers who sacrificed life and limb to rescue others? Or the way people, many still in shock themselves, rushed to give blood in makeshift donor banks?

This day of infamy immediately sent shock waves around the world. Most of us remember where we were when we first heard the news. I was standing in a second-hand bookstore in southern Spain. I remember people around me talking in hushed and sombre tones, but I couldn't quite catch what they were saying. The store's owner was telling someone that the US authorities were hoping there'd be no more attacks. I left the store and rushed back to my hotel. My wife and I had been taking a few days' break together, our first alone together in a long time. We turned on the news. It was hard to believe. We sat watching the news coverage for the most of the afternoon, stunned. Afterwards, we prayed.

Prophetic People . . .

It is a basic tenet of Bible revelation that God is able to bring hope out of despair, to turn trauma into triumph, to bring healing out of immense pain. The prophet Isaiah reminds us of this:

> *[God will] bestow on them [his people] a crown of beauty instead of ashes, the oil of gladness instead of mourning, and a garment of praise instead of a spirit of despair. (Isaiah 61:3)*

Pioneer Passion

It is also true that whenever God is about to do something significant in the world he first reveals his intentions to the people who trust in him, to his community of faith. When God responds to events like those of September 11, he speaks his word to the church because he wants to work through it to the world.

The famed evangelist T. L. Osborn once told me: 'I believe in reincarnation. In a sense, every time a person comes to Christ the Word becomes flesh all over again.' Of course, he was well aware that this statement could easily be misunderstood. But it *is* true that all Christians, through their lives of faith and trust, make Jesus real to their friends and acquaintances.

Throughout history, God's favourite means of communication has been incarnation. He wraps his transcendent, eternal truth in human form and experience so that it is accessible to us. By dressing truth in 'human clothes', he brings it to my level of understanding, to a place where I can touch it and relate to it. I can see how the truth fits my life – or, rather, how I should fit my life into the truth!

This, by the way, is one reason why Christian people go through tough times. Usually, the first thing we say when confronted with a trial of some kind is: 'What are you trying to teach me, Lord?' And that's a valid question – there's always something we can discover about God's will and his ways. Usually, we can learn something about ourselves, too. Sometimes our trials reveal our weaknesses; sometimes they show up our strengths. They throw light on reserves of faith and endurance that God has been working into our lives. Times of pressure reveal inner, spiritual resources we didn't know we possessed.

Yet, when we are sometimes called to leave the hilltops for the valleys it may also be for the sake of others and what *they* can learn about God. The singer Joan Osborne

18 *The Pioneer Spirit*

spoke for a generation when she poignantly asked, 'What if God was one of us?' How would God respond if he were in my shoes? What difference would his faith, hope and love make in my existential situation?

For people who do not yet know him, God sometimes answers this question through the experience of friends who do. In the midst of their real life challenges, God points them toward colleagues, friends or acquaintances who live by faith in him and who, though they face the same kinds of challenges, rise above them through the power of his Spirit. 'You want to know what I look like in your situation?' God asks. 'Take a look at that Christian friend of yours. He's in much the same boat sometimes, yet look at the faith, the hope, the love he has! That's what I can do in *your* life.'

God did not instigate the events of September 11. That tragedy was the product of depraved human hearts and minds that not only ignored what God is like, but had also forgotten what it means to be truly human. In the midst of the horror, though, God is able to create something positive out of the painful ruins.

Christians are God's prophetic people. If Christians are to have influence in this post-modern world, it will not be because of our ability to celebrate the past. Influence will come from our capacity to shape the future, in line with God's purposes. If we are listening to God's voice and adjusting our lives to fit his plans, we will belong to a community that is collectively able to identify and announce God's preferred future before it happens. More on that in coming chapters . . .

Christians are the ones who, above all others can reveal the new insights God wants to bring from old scars. There *is* something God wants to say to the post-9/11 world. Christians are the ones who need to discover it and announce it, giving leadership and pioneering a new way forward.

A Call to Passion!

The effects of September 11, 2001 were felt at a deeper level than just the emotion of the moment. They left people throughout the world with much to think about and work through for a long while after.

I think that perhaps the greatest impact for people the world over was this: the whole event threw into sharp relief the blandness, the lack of passion with which most of us conduct our daily lives.

Until now, ours has been the age of bland. 'Our machines are disturbingly lively,' wrote feminist philosopher Donna Haraway, 'and we ourselves frighteningly inert.'[2]

The post-modern age of political correctness has produced a generation that has made being inoffensive its greatest virtue. Post-modern thinking has taught us that all versions of reality are equally genuine, that all lifestyles are equally valid. We have been taught that it's okay to believe that something is true, as long as you don't insist that is *the* truth of the matter.

Leonard Sweet makes an interesting observation about how this is reflected in our news media. Legendary American broadcaster Walter Cronkite used to end each evening's newscast with the words, 'And that's the way it is.' The next generation's Dan Rather, on the other hand, will close off with the less certain, 'Well, that's part of our world tonight . . .'[3]

Until now, people of this generation have been walking around on eggshells. We've been trying so hard not to stand on anyone else's toes – to the point of confusing political correctness with truth. The secular world has been preaching 'blessed are the comfortable'. Some of the church has responded with nothing more than 'comfortable are the blessed'. All this has led to the death of passion.

20 *The Pioneer Spirit*

Yet, in the wake of that day in September, in the face of Ground Zero, people seem to be less willing to call everything 'negotiable'. Some things, it seems, clearly *are* wrong and evil. Some things, like freedom, are true and *worth* fighting passionately to defend. Events have shaken our comfortable maintenance mentality. Whether we like it or not, the boat of our complacency has been rocked. We need to face up to the real world of good and evil; we need to pioneer new and more definite ways of moving forward.

For Christians, there should be at least one major lesson learned from that fateful day. We can no longer afford to present a 'business-as-usual', 'more-of-the-same' face to the world. We must meet people with a zeal for our God that is greater than their passion for their gods – whatever they may be. The church must do more than mirror the status quo. It must offer a commitment that outlasts all others, a hope that is not founded upon the whims of fate and a way forward that really works.

For the church, if for no other group, September 11 surely represented the death of blandness and a call to passion. The church, like the secular culture it is called to serve and lead, needs a revival of passionate living and leadership!

Even a cursory scan through the Bible shows us that the God revealed there is a passionate God. He is anything but the clinical and emotionless – yes, even 'nice' – figure the church has sometimes represented him to be. He is a zealous God.

Moses, the great prophet and architect of Israel's nationhood, reminded us of this when he celebrated Israel's deliverance from Egypt:

I will sing to the Lord, for he is highly exalted. The horse and its rider he has hurled into the sea. The Lord is my

Pioneer Passion

*strength and my song; he has become my salvation. He is
my God, and I will praise him, my father's God, and I will
exalt him. The LORD is a warrior; the LORD is his name.
(Exodus 15:1–3)*

The people of Israel were throwing a party following the
overthrow of Egypt's army. They had suffered many
things while living under Pharaoh's rule. They might
have expected that, when God heard their pleas for help
and raised up a deliverer, their misery would be
alleviated. In fact, the opposite happened. Whenever
Moses brought the word of the Lord to 'let my people go',
the heart of Pharaoh became even more embittered
toward them and their anguish was intensified.[4]

At the time, the people of Israel could not see the point
in all the opposition they were facing. They couldn't
understand why God was allowing the king's heart to be
continually hardened. Later, though, in the challenging
days of their exodus and the conquest of Canaan, they
could look back and be assured of the greatness of their
God.

Before God sent his people out of Egypt, he displayed
his awesome greatness at Pharaoh's expense, so that he
could display the power of his name. Every plague God
sent on Egypt was also a direct challenge to a particular
Egyptian deity. Why send frogs on Egypt? Because frogs
were part of the Egyptian religion. Why locusts? Because
they also featured in Egyptian rites. God was not only
displaying his authority over Pharaoh, but over every
false god the Egyptians had conceived. His passion for
his people and his name were so great that even the
mightiest kings on earth – and the greatest gods of men –
could not withstand him.

The Israelites could gain confidence by looking back
on those events. When they did, they were reminded that

22 *The Pioneer Spirit*

theirs was a God who would not share his glory with another. Theirs was a God who could bring them through anything. Theirs was a God who demonstrated his right to receive worship – and he did it in such a definitive, 'watch this' kind of way! Moses later summed this up again, when he said to Israel:

> *For the LORD your God is a consuming fire, a jealous God. (Deuteronomy 4:24)*

God's zeal is in not the fanatical, myopic fervour that drives the murderous zealot. It is the joyful passion of a God who takes pleasure in his work and his people. It is the totally righteous, protective love felt by a father for his children, or a husband for his wife. The prophet Zephaniah took up this theme:

> *The LORD your God is with you, he is mighty to save. He will take great delight in you, he will quiet you with his love, he will rejoice over you with singing. (Zephaniah 3:17)*

If you read this in a Hebrew version of the Bible, you'll see that it carries much more emotion than our insipid English translations. It says that God wants to spin around us under the influence of violent emotion!

In the Old Testament, the zeal or passion of God is one of the great motivations behind everything he does. It causes him to keep a remnant of his people, even if most of them have turned away from him.[5] It leads him to establish an everlasting kingdom for his Son.[6] It moves him to give the righteous an inheritance in the face of opposition.[7] And it motivates him to judge and triumph over his enemies.[8]

Holy, Holy, Holy

In the eyes of some people, Christians are invaders from the planet Nerd; weird beings that have come to earth speaking a language that nobody really understands. According to this view, Christians have one goal: to bore everyone else into helpless submission. For people who see Christianity that way, becoming a Christian is about as desirable as being mutated into a Mr Bean clone!

That's *not* what Christianity is about. Christians are called to be different, but not weird! They are supposed to be 'separated' from the world, but never isolated from it. What the Bible calls holiness has nothing to do with being bland, colourless or uninteresting.

The book of Revelation gives us a glimpse right into the holiest place in heaven itself. In chapter four, the apostle John is taken in his vision through a doorway that leads to the throne room of God. His eyes are focussed upon a group of majestic beings. They constantly worship before the presence of God. John obviously finds it difficult to express what he sees:

Also before the throne there was what looked like a sea of glass, clear as crystal. In the centre, around the throne, were four living creatures, and they were covered with eyes, in front and behind. The first living creature was like a lion, the second was like an ox, the third had a face like a man, the fourth was like a flying eagle. (Revelation 4:6–7)

Poor John – imagine trying to put heaven into earthbound pictures! What follows is one of the most powerful texts in the Bible, and one that has inspired countless hymns and other songs through the ages:

Each of the four living creatures had six wings and was

covered with eyes all around, even under his wings. Day and night they never stop saying: 'Holy, holy, holy is the Lord God Almighty, who was, and is, and is to come.' (Revelation 4:8)

Often, when people find themselves surprised by some act of kindness, some unexpected good deed, they respond with something like, 'I don't know what to say . . .' Yet, in most cases, they quickly find their voice again and can't wait to express themselves.

In John's amazing vision, the angels closest to the throne of God possess an intelligence we can only dream of and a beauty we can only imagine. These magnificent beings are so awe-inspiring that John can't find words adequate to describe them. They are so wonderful that, if we didn't know better, we might consider them gods in their own right. Yet, these wondrous creatures are constantly taken aback by the magnificence and the awe-inspiring beauty of God's glory. Despite the fact that they spend all their time looking at him, they're continually taken aback by what they see. So much so, that they can only shield their eyes and utter one word over and over again – 'Holy, holy, holy . . .'

In many parts of the church, 'holy' has come to mean 'bland'. Many people imagine all churches to be places filled with bland music, bland preaching and bland programmes. But the angelic beings in heaven know better. They know what holiness *really* means. True holiness confronts you with someone who is so far above what you were expecting, so far beyond what you're ready to receive, that his presence knocks the wind and the words right out of you! God's presence literally takes your breath away.

That's why Paul tells us that:

Pioneer Passion

God can do anything . . . far more than you could ever imagine or guess or request in your wildest dreams! (Ephesians 3:20, The Message)

In God, holiness and passion are intertwined. John Eldredge is right when he says that, 'The greatest enemy of holiness is not passion; it is apathy.'[9] Buckminster Fuller, the famed architect and inventor, suggested that the basic purpose of people on earth is to counteract the tide of entropy, the process by which things naturally wind down. We were designed to keep things 'on the boil', by a God who is himself a zealous person!

Sin is not the release of passion, but the *abuse* of passion – directing it toward a wrong, or ungodly end. Truly godly people are anything but uninspiring or uninteresting people. Those who worship a holy God are more alive to life's incredible adventure than anyone else, because their greatest role model is so amazing that he takes your breath away!

Jesus, Man of Passion

In one of my earlier books, *Burning Questions,* I wrote that when some people think of God they're immediately reminded of the Father Mulcahy character from the TV series *M*A*S*H*. Mulcahy's a nice man and he definitely means well, but he's not what you'd call a get-things-done kind of guy. If you needed help with some pressing problem, you wouldn't go to Mulcahy; you'd head for Hawkeye Pierce, the wisecracking chief surgeon who has life and passion oozing out of his fingertips.

Many people imagine Jesus to be a kind of caftan-wearing Father Mulcahy. He's good-hearted and generous, but hardly the kind of person you want in your corner if push comes to shove. The fact is, though, that the Jesus of history was far from bland or business-as-usual. The novelist Dorothy Sayers has expressed this brilliantly.

'The people who hanged Christ never . . . accused Him of being a bore,' she says. 'On the contrary; they thought Him too dynamic to be safe. It has been left for later generations to muffle up that shattering personality and surround Him with an atmosphere of tedium.'

She goes on: 'We have effectively pared the claws of the Lion of Judah, certified Him "meek and mild" and recommended Him as a fitting household pet for pale curates and pious old ladies.

'To those who knew Him, however, He in no way suggested a milk-and-water person; they objected to Him as a dangerous firebrand. True, He was tender to the unfortunate, patient with honest inquirers, and humble before Heaven, but He insulted respectable clergymen by calling them hypocrites; He referred to King Herod as "that fox"; He went to parties in disreputable company and was looked upon as a "gluttonous man and a wine bibber, a friend of publicans . . ."

'[He] assaulted indignant tradesmen and threw them and their belongings out of the Temple; He drove a coach-and-horses through a number of sacrosanct and hoary regulations; He cured diseases by any means that came handy, with a shocking casualness in the matter of other people's pigs and property . . .'

Finally, Sayers arrives at this conclusion: '[Jesus] was emphatically not a dull man in His human lifetime, and if He was God, there can be nothing dull about God either.'[10]

You don't have to take Dorothy Sayers' word for it. The record is there in the gospels; you can check it for yourself. When Jesus was asked what constituted the greatest commandment, he replied with these words:

Pioneer Passion

The first in importance is, 'Listen, Israel: The Lord your God is one; so love the Lord God with all your passion and prayer and intelligence and energy.' And here is the second: 'Love others as well as you love yourself.' (Mark 12:29–31, The Message)

According to Jesus, our first priority in life should be to release all of our passion in the service of God.

Jesus' own way of living was so zealous and animated that his personality could seem, at best, unpredictable. One day, Jesus told his leading disciple, Peter, that he'd been blessed with special revelation from God. Then, just a short while later, Jesus was full of reproach for Peter. 'Out of my sight, Satan,' he said.[11] Peter must have felt mortified, and more than a little uncertain of himself from then on.

If you heard Jesus preach, you might describe him as abrupt. He didn't mind treading on respectable toes, with quotable quotes like, 'Woe to you who are rich and well fed . . .'[12] You might even say that Jesus was aggressive, especially if you happened to be on the receiving end of one of his temple-trading tirades![13]

I suppose that, at worst, you might see Jesus as downright arrogant – which is how some of his enemies liked to describe him. They *thought* they heard him say, 'Tear down this temple of Herod that's taken you forty-six years to build. In three days, I will raise it up again.' The impudence of the man! (What he actually said was quite different, but they weren't going to let the facts stand in the way of a good story.)[14] It was during one of his more enthusiastic outbursts that his followers remembered a prophecy given about him. It said, 'Zeal for your house will consume me!'[15]

Throughout his busy life of ministry, Jesus was far too busy being *prophetically* correct to be *politically* correct. He

28 *The Pioneer Spirit*

was well aware of what lukewarm spirituality meant in the eyes of a zealous God.

Much later, the apostle John was given a taste of how Jesus felt toward lukewarm spirituality. In his vision on Patmos, John was given a very direct message for some Christians who were leading indifferent lives. They were neither cold nor hot in their faith, which prompted Jesus to say to them: 'You make me want to vomit.'[16]

Let's face it: there are people and situations all around us that conspire to steal away our zeal. We are surrounded by a world that is drunk with fashionable conventions and politically correct thinking. The style police want to tell us what we can and can't think or feel and a humanistic world-view tries to squeeze from us all excitement about sharing our faith. True pioneers, however, are passionate people. They will not accept a life devoid of zeal. They refuse to allow the bland customs of this world to sap their drive, their emotional energy. They learn to keep the inner fires burning, to use their devotion to higher things as a motivation to break new ground. They live to create breakthroughs for themselves and for others.

How do we revive passionate living and keep our zeal alive? We begin by learning to live with hunger.

Living with Hunger

Sometimes, it's good to see the old John 3:16 posters held up at football games. At least somebody is trying to get Jesus' message to the masses. Yet, the message about Jesus can't really be boiled down to one or two favourite Bible texts. The gospel, the good news, is a complete world-view, a way of seeing reality or explaining the way things are in the world.

The Christian world-view explains more fully than any other philosophical system why the world is as it is, while giving us hope and a way forward for the future. It tells us who – and whose – we are, where we came from and where we are going. The Christian world-view is very different from others. This is true, for example, of the Christian assessment of human life. Christians value life as a sacred gift entrusted to us by God. Because we are stewards of this gift, it is not something we should lightly seek to destroy, whether in wars or in laboratories.

Christians also see human life as being more than a temporal thing. According to the Bible, death is not the end of us. When this life ends, another one begins. So our present decisions carry ramifications not only for time, but also for eternity. This elevates human will and responsibility to a very high level. It also means that our decisions in the here-and-now can create a long-lasting legacy for good. We *can* create something that lives on when we die!

Until fairly recently, people in the West tended to live with a purely materialistic, naturalistic view of human existence. Knowingly or not, they tended to swallow the teachings of men like Darwin in the field of biology, and Descartes in the arena of philosophy. They accepted that human beings are simply the result of natural or environmental processes; that people lack a higher, moral soul; and that our bodies are our property to do with as we please. Of course, in the last few years people have shown a growing interest in all things spiritualistic – from ghosts, to so-called 'white' witchcraft. There is also a genuine interest in Christian faith – especially when people see God's power at work in miraculous ways. Yet, in spite of this interest in the supernatural, materialistic thinking still maintains a powerful grip on our moral choices.

The Pioneer Spirit

Because our western culture has tried to throw off its Christian heritage and value system, life in our world is increasingly devalued and demystified. We have managed, for example, to strip sex of its spiritual and moral aspects. We've made it out to be little more than a fun experience, a little personal indulgence to be shared between friends – or even just acquaintances. We have deprived childhood of dignity and value, too. Pro-abortionists see the foetus as being little more than bodily tissue. A woman, they say, has the final and sole right to decide what happens to the unborn child who is 'taking up space' inside her body.

Having lost our reverence for life, we've also lost much of our respect for death. Today, some people argue that death is just another 'lifestyle option'. Euthanasia is being legalized in some supposedly civilized nations because, so the thinking goes, people have the right to use their bodies as they wish. Actually, euthanasia is not giving a person the right to die; it's giving one person the right to take the life of another!

The Bible teaches that our bodies are not, in the end, our property at all. We owe the very existence of our bodies to God. We do have certain rights as to how we treat our bodies, but those rights must be exercised within the safe parameters *he* has laid down.

All around us, people are adopting a world-view that is slowly but surely tying us to a culture of death. There is, however, a moral and spiritual aspect to our lives and we will be held accountable for the way we treat bodies. Because human life is a bequest from God, Christians have stood to protest whenever societies have tried to tear down the sanctity of life.

C. S. Lewis once made the point that if human life can be measured in terms of just seventy years or so, then a state, nation or civilisation is more important than an

Pioneer Passion 31

individual person as a nation may last for a thousand years. But, if Christianity is correct and human existence is both spiritual and eternal, then an individual human being is much more valuable than a state. The human individual has everlasting life, while the life of the civilisation, by comparison, lasts only for a moment.

Human life *is* an eternal thing – and there's an interesting corollary to this. Because I was built for eternity, my present life in time and space will always carry a certain amount of frustration for me. As long as I am in this body, I will feel a deep yearning for things that I can never fully experience in this life.

Nothing kills passion in our lives like unresolved frustration. Frustration comes when my expectation exceeds my experience, when I reach for something great but receive something less.

Frustration can spring from a number of sources. For example, I might be frustrated because I have failed at something. If the failure is a moral or ethical one, I should confess, repent, forgive myself and then try to repair any damage to relationships. Then I should move on. Sometimes, I become frustrated by the failure of other people. When somebody lets me down, I need to acknowledge the hurt, forgive the person, and then move on.

Sometimes, I get frustrated because of impatience with God's timetable. God doesn't wear a Rolex – sometimes he seems to respond very slowly to my very urgent pleas for help. In cases like that, I must learn to do what the psalmist said: 'Be still before the Lord and wait patiently for him.'[17] Then, when he gives me the go-ahead, I can move on.

There is another major source of frustration in life; one for which there is no easy remedy. I can get very restless if I want in the here-and-now what only heaven can provide. In that case, I can't move on. I must learn to accommodate the hunger, even to appreciate it.

The Pioneer Spirit

Pascal said that, 'We are never living, but hoping to live; and whilst we are always preparing to be happy, it is certain, we never shall be so, if we aspire to no other happiness than what can be enjoyed in this life.'[18] G. K. Chesterton put it this way: '[This] is what makes life at once so splendid and so strange. The true happiness is that we don't fit. We come from somewhere else.'[19] U2 expressed it in a song: 'I still haven't found what I'm looking for . . .'

In a world where we are encouraged to fill every hunger *now*, to achieve immediate gratification for every need, it is healthy for us to remember that we are in the world, but not of it.[20]

Sometimes, we're like the lame man who sat by the pool in John chapter five. The waters were rumoured to have special healing properties. Some people even claimed that an angel came and touched them, stirring them up so that people could be healed. Actually, the earliest manuscripts of this gospel don't make any mention of an angel. That part may have been just a local superstition. Perhaps these were natural springs, with natural healing properties. Whatever its source, though, the people believed in the transforming power of the waters. They thought that the first person into the pool when the waters were moving could be cured.

Off and on for thirty-eight years, the lame man had been coming to this pool, waiting to be healed. One day, Jesus met him there and asked if he was really serious about being cured. The man mumbled that he had nobody to carry him to the waters when they moved. Jesus ignored that completely. He looked the man right in the eye and said, 'Get up! Pick up your mat and walk.' Jesus knew that the bubbling waters were a cheap substitute for what he alone could provide – total healing, inside *and* out.

Pioneer Passion

There are times in our lives when we look longingly at the bubbling waters, believing that the things we really need are just within our reach. 'If I can just get that next job,' we say. 'If I can just meet that right partner . . . If I can just pull off that big deal . . . Then I'll be completely whole. Then I'll find what I'm hungry for.' The truth is, nothing we experience in this life will fully satisfy our most profound thirst. We were built for more than this life; we were constructed for heaven.

As long as you and I occupy these mortal bodies, we will suffer the effects of our fallenness. A part of us will always remain broken, waiting to be restored. You could have the greatest career or ministry on earth, and you would still not feel totally fulfilled. You could achieve the kind of success others only dream about, and you still wouldn't find complete satisfaction. You could meet the love of your life and have the most amazing, happy and enduring marriage, and you'd still have a hunger for intimacy.

All of these things are good in themselves. Through them, we can even get a *taste* of heaven in the here and now. That's what exercising faith in God's promises allows us to do: to get a sample of what's to come. The favour of God in this life – the working of his Holy Spirit to heal, protect and bless us – is like a deposit on the full balance that's to come.[21] Whenever we receive healing, financial blessing or any miracle, you know that this is what heaven will be like. Only, in heaven there'll be more of it!

When a person is healed or blessed in any way, I think God is smiling to himself and saying, 'You think that's great . . . Wait until you see the real thing!'

The enemy of our souls knows that we look forward to heaven, that we long for the full realisation of our salvation. If he can't kill our longing for heaven, he will

34 *The Pioneer Spirit*

try to seduce it. He'll try to entice us to spend our passion on worldly things. He'll offer us the bubbling of the waters – the waters of position, status, material success or fame, for example. All they do, though, is keep our eyes off the real answer – Jesus.

In this life, I can enjoy God's rich bounty in a thousand ways every day but I must not get my roots down too deep. John Eldredge writes: 'God must take away the heaven we create, or it will become our hell . . . some deep and tender part of us gets trapped there in those times and places where we have had a taste of the life we long for . . . It's as if the golden center of my heart is back there in those golden days, and God wants to free it from there . . . [and to] bring it into the present for the future.'[22]

Even with all the blessings that this life has to offer – with all the benefits of God's promises and the power of answered prayers – I am still a stranger in a strange land. Like the patriarchs and prophets of old, I am 'longing for a better country – a heavenly one.'[23]

The very best experiences this world has to offer will only ever be an echo of a better life to come. This world is not my home. There may be a level of frustration attached to that fact, but it's a feeling I can turn to my advantage. Instead of trying to smother it with money, position or worldly success, I can use it to fuel my prayers and to motivate me toward a bolder life of faith and risk.

Learning to live with my hunger for heaven – to see it for what it is – can help me release the pioneer spirit. It can drive me to commit my life to something that lives on when I die!

Pioneer Passion

1. Leonard I. Sweet, *SoulTsunami* (Zondervan Publishing House, 1999), p. 110
2. Quoted, ibid., p. 190
3. Ibid., p. 109
4. Exodus 8:15, 32; 9:12, 34; 10:1, 20, 27
5. 2 Kings 19:31
6. Isaiah 9:7
7. Isaiah 26:11
8. Ezekiel 36:5 and Isaiah 42:13
9. John Eldredge, *The Journey of Desire* (Thomas Nelson, 2000), p. 54
10. Quoted by Howard Hendricks, *Color Outside The Lines* (Word Publishing, 1998), pp. 14, 15
11. Matthew 16:23
12. Luke 6:24–25
13. John 2:13–16
14. Cf. John 2:19–22
15. John 2:17 and Psalm 69:9
16. Revelation 3:16, *The Message*
17. Psalm 37:7
18. Quoted by John Eldredge, op cit., p. 104
19. Quoted, ibid., p. 12
20. Cf. John 17:14
21. Ephesians 1:14
22. John Eldredge, op cit., p. 100
23. Hebrews 11:16

3

Designing the Future

It is AD 401. Patricius, a sixteen-year-old boy, is working at his home in Roman England.

Suddenly, a band of marauding Irish warriors appears from nowhere and, before he knows it, Patricius is snatched away as a slave. He is sold to a small-time Irish chieftain, who sends him out to shepherd his flocks.

There in the fields, under a constantly changing Irish sky, young Pat must fight hunger and cold weather in a constant battle to stay alive. Alone and afraid, he thinks back on his upbringing, and how his parents had taught him about the Christian God.

He has always thought of Christian priests as total fools. He decided as a boy that he would have nothing to do with the Christian faith. Now, though, he sits in sad isolation, yearning for home. So he begins to pray and finds in God a strength he's never experienced before.

One night, he is awakened from his slumber by a voice that tells him he is going home, that there's a ship waiting to carry him there. He sets off for the sea and, more than two hundred miles later, he finds a ship headed for England.

When he sets foot on home soil, after years away, he

Designing the Future 37

finds that he can't fit in with his own people. In the midst of his restlessness, he hears the voice again, the voice of Christ. This time, it tells him he will one day return to Ireland – not this time as a slave, but as a Christian missionary.

After theological training, he returns to the land of the Irish with a new name – Patrick. There he faces fierce opposition from pagan priests, who still use human sacrifices to try to appease their Celtic gods. Among his parishioners are Irish warriors who still hang from their belts the skulls of their enemies. Yet, despite his inauspicious beginnings, Patrick goes on to become one of the saviours of Western civilisation, a truly prophetic pioneer.

Patrick – or, as we know him, St Patrick – established monasteries across Ireland. These centres of Christian mission eventually brought peace to a land ravaged by inter-tribal strife. More than that, they sent out Christian pioneers who revolutionized the known world.

It was Patrick and his followers who exchanged the values of a warrior society for the peaceful principles of Christianity. Patrick and his fellow monks kept alive both Christianity and Western civilisation, when internal decadence and external barbarianism threatened to wipe both from the face of the earth.

Patrick's monks copied every book they could get their hands on, including the classics of Greek and Rome, and they taught their converts Latin, music and painting. They infused new life into Christianity with their profound respect for and love of the Bible. 'Between AD 650 and 850,' writes Charles Colson, 'more than half of all known biblical commentaries were written by Irishmen.'[1]

Because of the unfailing efforts of Patrick's evangelists, even the bloodthirsty barbarians eventually exchanged their weapons for farming tools and peace finally came to Europe. John Henry Newman says that, because of the influence of the monasteries, 'the woody swamp became a hermitage, a religious house, a farm, an abbey, a village, a seminary, a school of learning, a city.'[2]

'Within St Patrick's lifetime,' Colson writes, 'warriors cast aside their swords of battle, intertribal warfare decreased markedly, and the slave trade ended. A culture of battle and brute power was transformed by an ethic that sanctified manual labour, poverty, and service. A culture of illiteracy and ignorance became a culture of learning.'

'This,' he adds, 'is how Christianity is meant to function in society – not just as a private faith but as a creative force in the culture . . . In every choice and decision we make . . . we either help build a life-giving, peace-loving ethos, or fan the flames of egoism and destruction.'[3]

The Future Before it Happens

In his challenging books, such as *New Thinking for the New Millennium*, Edward de Bono suggests that it is possible to 'design the future' by making good choices in the present and by changing the way we learn to think.

'[Traditionally] we seek to solve problems,' he says, 'by identifying the cause and then seeking to remove that cause . . . In practice, it is not quite so simple. It may not be easy to isolate the cause. Most of the world's major problems will not be solved by further analysis. The problems have been analysed enough already. What we need to do is to "design a way forward" . . .'[4]

Allan Kaye, one of the developers of the now ubiquitous PC, has said, 'the best way to control the

Designing the Future

future is to invent it.' Other writers have said that to shape the future we must understand it before it happens. That has always been the role of pioneer thinkers throughout the ages – to design a way forward for others, a path toward a better future.

The laser was invented by Gordon Gould and is now an integral part of many technologies and tools. The CD player was created by James Russell and is now a common part of everyday life. Marcian Hoff, the inventor of the microchip, opened up the true potential of computing and Tim Berners Lee, creator of the World Wide Web, put the power of the Internet within easy reach of us all.

Someone has said that a genius is someone who alters our perception of reality. People like these did more than analyse existing problems. They launched techniques and technologies that actually created a whole new way of doing things. They built a bridge to tomorrow, by helping to shape how the future would look.

As followers of Christ, we are called not simply to live in history. We are destined to *change* history. We are called to shape the future before it arrives, working in the here-and-now world to point people toward the Kingdom of God. After all, within each of us resides the same Spirit that caused a carpenter-cum-rabbi, who came from a country town of no more than five hundred people, to change history forever – in just three years!

Christians are prophetic people. That doesn't mean they float around above the rest of humanity, never being touched by worldly concerns and quoting obscure Scriptures at all and sundry. People like that are not spiritual, they're just insecure. Truly prophetic people are marked by several characteristics.

1. Prophetic people see the present in the light of God's preferred future

Truly prophetic people understand their own times; they see the present as God sees it, in the light of his coming kingdom.

Sometimes, when you're reading a story, you understand the middle better when you've come to the end. Knowing how things turn out and who wins and loses can help you better appreciate the actions and events along the way. It's the same with history. If you understand something of the end of the story, you will be able to make more sense of the middle.

In the Bible, God has already *shown* us the end of history. He has revealed the future, and the future is the Kingdom of God. One day, the kingdoms of this world will become part of the dominion of Christ.[5] This unveiling of Jesus' kingdom will constitute the culmination of world history and the world will find lasting peace under its umbrella. Jesus will reign on earth not because he has been elected to do so, but because he alone is *worthy* and able to do so.

The new-world kingdom will incorporate people from every ethnic group on earth, redeeming the cultures and bringing them to their ultimate expression.[6] This kingdom will thrive on the values Jesus gave us through his life and ministry, principles that are summed up, for example, in the Sermon on the Mount.[7] That sermon was much more than just a nice homily on healthy living and relationships – it was a declaration of the constitutional values of Jesus' coming kingdom. It was a statement of how the future will look!

Dr Martin Luther King made one of his most memorable speeches near the end of his life. Standing before a packed church in Memphis, he said, 'I don't know what will happen to me now. We've got some

Designing the Future

difficult days ahead. But it doesn't matter to me now, because I've been to the mountaintop. I won't mind. Like anybody else, I would like to live a long life.

'Longevity has its place. But I'm not concerned about that now. I just want to do God's will. And He's allowed me to go up to the mountain. And I've looked over and seen the Promised Land. I may not get there with you, but I want you to know tonight that we, as a people, will get to the Promised Land. I'm happy tonight . . . I'm not fearing any man. "Mine eyes have seen the glory of the coming of the Lord." '[8]

These are brave words. Shortly after making this speech, King was gunned down outside his hotel room and the world lost one of its greatest, yet most peaceable revolutionaries. Revd King was able to affect the future because he understood the present, not just from the point of view of sociology, economics or politics, but in the light of the Kingdom of God. He lined up the present with what he knew of the teaching and ministry of Jesus. His dream was really a call for people to live by the values of Jesus' kingdom. He saw with certainty where the journey of history would ultimately end – so he was able to boldly engage the present.

The influence of the church does not come from its ability to celebrate the past, but from its capacity to shape the future. Each of us can call God's preferred future into existence in the present, by lining up our choices with the choices God would make about us and our world.

Right now, Christians should be seeking to shape the future in a major way, living out God's kingdom in the present. We may feel like we're in the minority right now but, in the long run, kingdom living will become the *majority* lifestyle. When we live day-to-day according to the values of God's kingdom, we are declaring the shape of the future before it happens. *We are living in the future before it arrives.*

42 *The Pioneer Spirit*

2. *Prophetic people speak God's future word into 'now' situations*

Because prophetic people see the future – the Kingdom of God – they are able to speak God's future word into now situations.

Across the world today, there's a growing move to plant contemporary churches. Riga, Latvia is a city of just one million people and the capital of a nation of just two million. A little over a decade ago, the nation was under communist rule and freedom of religion was just a distant dream. Many pastors were thrown into prison for their faith.

Not too long ago, I was able to speak in a church of over two thousand people in this city. To say that I was impressed with what I saw would be an understatement. Now, I have the privilege of speaking in some of the finest churches around. But I have to tell you: you'd go a long way to find better music in any church, anywhere!

These people have brought together house music, jazz-fusion and rock 'n' roll in a cutting-edge blend of sounds. They've also produced rock musicals that retell the story of Jesus, placing it firmly in the context of modern life in the Russian-speaking world. And when digital camera cranes sweep over the Sunday crowd, you can see the church's strong commitment to outreach through sophisticated electronic media. All of the technology, though, is just a servant to the overriding sense of God's presence in the house. People are healed and delivered and God is made famous among his people.

This is just one of the many thousands of truly contemporary churches that are springing up across the globe. They're exciting, they're user-friendly and they're growing fast. Looking just at the surface level, some observers might say that the secret of their success is their hip style. But it goes deeper than that: being

Designing the Future

contemporary is something that must be born in the heart of the leader, something that informs his or her entire approach to ministry. Unless the leader has the spirit of a pioneer, no amount of tweaking the weekly programme, or re-writing its constitution will ever attract new people to the church.

The word 'contemporary' means 'to exist at the same time'. When we say that Winston Churchill and Adolf Hitler were contemporaries, we do not mean that they had much in common. We mean that they lived through the same era.

For a long time, much of the church in the West seems to have been cocooned from reality inside a kind of time warp. Somehow, the church has managed to communicate that it is more comfortable maintaining the past than initiating change in the future. The church has lived in a bygone era, remembering perceived glory days when – supposedly – everyone respected the church and what it had to offer. In our time, though, God is raising up churches and leaders that are working hard to inhabit the *real* world, to speak where people are listening. Thank God for that!

However, in the midst of our drive to create a contemporary expression of faith, we must keep one important thing in focus. Being contemporary is a *means to an end*, not an end in itself. Being contemporary means that we are relevant, or in touch with our times. But the real goal should always be that we become *prophetic*, ahead of the times. Contemporary styles and thinking simply provide us with the vocabulary to announce God's preferred future before it arrives.

3. Prophetic people produce models of change – to demonstrate what the future looks like

For a long time, parts of the Western church have been satisfied to emulate what the world does, to mirror the status quo. We've produced 'Christian TV', 'Christian magazines' and a 'Christian music industry'. Too often, we've tried to talk to our world using nothing more than secular models to which we've added the tag 'Christian'. We've failed to invent anything better, anything fresh, and consequently the world has ignored us. Our real calling is to set up alternatives to the status quo, to do things in brave *new* ways.

When I was younger (so much younger than today . . .), I had a bike with trainer wheels. Those little trainers attached to the back wheel allowed me to push forward boldly, without fear of falling off. I felt secure, though I was doing something I'd never attempted before.

The church should be providing trainer wheels to propel people into the future. People should look at Christians and say, 'When I'm watching you guys, I feel secure about pushing forward. You help me see that the future can be a place of hope and new beginnings.'

When the preacher George Whitefield initiated a school to train African–Americans for employment, he didn't simply copy secular programmes of the day. There *were* none. His school was built seventy years *before* emancipation, before slaves could even think about getting jobs. His bold, new initiative was far from popular in many places, but it *was* prophetic because it modelled a better future before it happened.

When William Wilberforce stood in the British Parliament to declare slavery abhorrent and immoral, his words fell for a long time on deaf ears. What he was advocating represented a major challenge to the money

Designing the Future

interests of the day. Yet he and his small group of supporters persisted and, over many years, they announced God's preferred future before it occurred.

God gave great favour to men like Whitefield and Wilberforce because they were prepared to do more than emulate the world in which they lived. They thought and acted in a prophetic way. When they knew what the future *should* look like, they spoke God's word into the present and set up models to show how it could be carried out.

God will never give his future word to churches, organisations or individuals who are unwilling – or unable – to spread that word around. God is looking for people like Daniel who can see with the eye of the prophet, yet speak with the tongue of the people. He is looking for people who hear from heaven but speak the languages of this earth. Daniel was known as a man in whom 'the spirit of the gods' resided. Why? Because he could translate the mandates of heaven *into* the language of the Babylonians!

Speaking in many different parts of the world, I often rely heavily on the gifts and the skill of translators. What do translators do? They provide vocabulary in the context of locality. If a translator hears what I say and simply repeats it using the same words, the ideas themselves will still have power but they won't produce any change in the hearers. Translators must use their creativity to put my ideas into words that the local people can understand and use.

That's what God wants to do through his church – to declare the future in the here-and-now, in a way that makes sense to contemporary generations. He wants us to provide a local vocabulary for his prophetic word.

A Future Redeemed

Much has been written and said about the importance of vision. The need for vision cannot be underestimated, in business, in ministry or in life itself. The Macquarie Dictionary defines vision as, 'the ability to perceive what is not visible to the naked eye.' Vision is an essential characteristic of all pioneers.

Helen Keller remarked that, 'The saddest thing [in life] is to have your sight yet have no vision.' According to Henry Ford, 'The poor man is not the man without a cent; he is the one without a dream.'

The Bible is very clear that 'without a vision the people perish.'[9] Vision keeps our lives focussed and on track; it adds discipline to our lives and provides parameters within which we can be truly creative. Without it, we 'run amok'.[10] When we have no vision, our lives are pulled in many directions at once, like horse-drawn carriages that have lost their drivers.

Yet, when the Bible talks about vision, it means something more than the personal goal-setting we read about in business books. Personal goals are a product of motivation: we set our goals according to what moves or excites us. Vision, in the spiritual sense, is the result of *revelation*. It begins in the heart of God, who then communicates it to us through the Bible, prophecy, circumstances and the wise counsel of leaders and friends.

Goals are our inventions and they lie within our control. Vision, though, comes from outside of us and takes hold of us – often, before we realize that it's happening. Goals are primarily about self-fulfilment, or the actualising of our own perceived potential. Jesus, however, told us to 'seek first the Kingdom of God.'[11] The word 'seek' is a vision word. It speaks of looking for

Designing the Future

something with determination, desire and focus. Real vision always carries implications for much more than self-realisation – it is about extending God's kingdom. It is about serving *his* interests, lining up our affections with *his* affections and seeing *his* rule extended, first in people's hearts and then in their relationships and in the institutions of which they are a part.

True vision is always *redemptive* in nature, too. The Amplified version of the Bible has a wonderful translation of Proverbs 29:18. It translates the word 'vision' as 'redemptive revelation'. That gives us a powerful lesson in what vision will do for us and through us: it will redeem, or buy back, ground that has been lost, to the Kingdom of God.

Vision does that because it contains a *revelation* of the nature and character of God. The revelation, if we work it out in our choices and actions, will redeem aspects of the world we live in. It will bring them back under God's influence.

If you are in business and your vision is to build a great company, you have a good goal, but it is not big enough! God wants you to have a redemptive revelation, a vision that leads to influence for his kingdom. He wants you to redefine what it means to be in business in your city.

If you are a student and your goal is simply to have a good career, your goal is too small for God. He wants to give you a vision for your life that will redefine what it means to be a student, and then what it means to be a professional in your field of choice. He wants you to change the culture in which you live, both on the local and the larger scale, both in the present and in the long-term future.

God has not called you simply to build him a company or a career, a ministry or even a family. *God has set you apart to build him a name!*

Vision Married to Strategy

Many well-meaning people look at the needs all around them and feel overwhelmed. They quickly decide that there is too much distress in the world, that there's nothing much they can do to change things. So, they settle back into passive living. Others try to do too much – and they burn out.

Need should never be our greatest motivator – we should be shaped first by vision or by the cause of the gospel. Jesus' works were not primarily motivated by human need but by obedience to the will of God.[12] On the cross, the Bible says, he saw beyond the moment and its shame to 'the joy set before him.'[13] The vision, the cause, gave him strength to endure the suffering. What motivated Jesus the most? It was the vision he shared with his Father – the plan for our salvation.

God-given vision is not an optional extra. If we are to live as innovative, breakthrough pioneers, it is essential. However, vision without strategy is nothing more than wishful thinking. Unless purposes are married to concrete plans, they take us no further than daydreams. Without strategies, we'll wander through life singing 'When You Wish Upon a Star' and achieving nothing!

Vision comes to help us redeem something for God's use. Every Christian ought, now and again, to ask themselves certain questions. If Jesus doesn't return within ten years, what kind of city or nation would I want to be living in then? What kind of business world would I want to work in? What kind of environment would I want my children to grow up in? What kind of church would I want to be a part of?

These forward-looking, long-range questions are strategic, because they lead us to formulate clear plans so that we can turn vision into redemptive reality.

Designing the Future 49

In any field, true pioneers tend to be strategic thinkers. They can project their thinking to see how the future *should* look, and then develop the steps that will take them there.

The Bible says that the church is built upon the foundation work of apostles and prophets.[14] These kinds of leaders have pioneer roles in the overall church. They work well in combination. Prophets can *see* a preferred future, while apostles are able to develop the plans and programmes to *get people there*. In combination, prophets and apostles can form great strategic teams.

I want to look more closely at what it means to think strategically. Before we talk about that, though, we need to agree on one thing: that we must *think* in the first place! Many Christians read Romans 12:2 this way: 'be transformed by the *removal* of your mind.' Actually, the Scriptures never suggest that a life of faith is a life devoid of careful thought and planning. In fact, the opposite is true. Consider these examples from the book of Proverbs alone:

The plans of the diligent lead to profit as surely as haste leads to poverty. (Proverbs 21:5)

Those who plan what is good find love and faithfulness. (Proverbs 14:22)

Commit to the LORD whatever you do, and your plans will succeed. (Proverbs 16:3)

Make plans by seeking advice . . . (Proverbs 20:18)

Some people imagine that the momentum of technology will make the ability to think, to plan, less important; that somehow our tools will do the thinking for us. This is

50 *The Pioneer Spirit*

wrong – and dangerous. 'The ability to send hundreds of emails,' writes de Bono, 'does not ensure the ability to write something intelligent or amusing. Having a fast car is not the same as having somewhere you want to go.'[15]

Your skin is renewed through cell regeneration every month. Your liver is renewed every six months, and your brain every twelve months. Think about that: having you think is *so important to God* that he gives you an upgraded brain every year!

Once you accept that thinking is important, you need to learn to think in a *strategic* way. Strategic thinking boldly engages the future. It uses its vision of the future to shape plans and programmes. It asks the big question: 'If I keep heading in this direction, where will I be in five years from now?' Or, 'If I want to get to this goal, what do I need to change here and now?'

Strategic planners are motivated to influence their environment more than it influences them. They are constructive rather than negative. They are pro-active people, instead of people who are infected with an 'I'm-just-a-product-of-my-environment' victim mentality.

Strategic thinking leads naturally to leadership. 'Creativity will develop our leadership potential,' writes Howard Hendricks. 'There is a strong correlation between creativity and leadership effectiveness. Leaders are visionaries, not people in a rut. They tend to see further, probe more deeply, and think with more insight than others.'[16]

It's Not Just What You Think, it's How You Think . . .

Increasingly, the focus in education is shifting away from just teaching people *what* to think towards teaching people *how* to think. In the past, schools have been well

Designing the Future

equipped to cram students' heads with data and facts. In today's information-saturated world, this kind of training is no longer adequate; it doesn't meet the need. The challenge for us is no longer just the *getting* of information, but knowing *what to do with* the plethora of messages we receive every day.

De Bono says, 'Information has a very important part to play in all thinking but no amount of information can take the place of new concepts and design thinking.'[17] People today need help to know how to sift the available information, responding to the important things decisively, creatively and quickly, and using information to create something of value.

In the past, education also focussed on the use of thinking processes to solve problems. This is no longer enough, either. In today's world – and the world of tomorrow – we must learn how to move *beyond* the analysis of existing problems to pre-empting possible outcomes in the future. Of course, that can sometimes sound suspiciously like teaching human beings that they can play God, but there *is* a truth here. We need to learn to think ahead, to look to the future with the freeing influence of hope, rather than the paralysing effect of anxiety.

This is particularly true of leaders, who are expected to see further over the horizon than their peers – and to know how to get there. In his book *How to Think*, Stephen Reid says: 'There are many ways and means to think, but without imagination life is an austere, bone-dry, dull place . . . If people are to be inspired to follow a great strategy, you will need the powers of imagination and self-expression.'[18]

In Acts 21, a group of prominent church leaders came to the apostle Paul and warned that if he made his way to Jerusalem, as planned, he would be bound and arrested. Paul's response was straightforward enough. 'I am ready,' he said.[19]

52 *The Pioneer Spirit*

In the English language, the word 'ready' has just the one meaning – to be prepared, to have done one's homework. That is not what Paul meant, though. The Greek word that's translated 'ready' here means to live in the future, or to be 'future-minded'. What is Paul saying? He's declaring, 'I am living in the future as if it is already happening.' That is the essence of strategic thinking: the ability to foresee events and to plan backwards from a desired goal. Being strategic means interacting with the future, in the present.

Christians ought to be better at strategic thinking than most other people are because faith, by definition, projects beyond present realities to grasp a better future. Faith links us with things we anticipate for tomorrow; faith puts substance on our future hopes.[20]

Rather than prophetically engaging the needy world around them, many Christians, sadly, prefer to settle back in the relative security of religious clichés and traditions. Consequently, the only Christians many post-modern westerners will encounter are those who know more about fantasy than faith.

Bill Wilson, the apostle to children, working in New York, has said, 'What you achieve in life is not as important as what you set in motion.' Strategic thinkers ask the question: 'What can I set in motion before I die? What lasting thing can I start that will live on when I am gone?'

Strategic thinking sees God's preferred future and starts the ball rolling *now*. It sees the promise of God and works backwards from that point in the future to this moment in time, making changes in the present to fit the promise.

Being strategic helps us to overcome fear. We often consume vast amounts of our limited energy reserves worrying over the future. Stephen Reid offers us some good advice here. 'I have found the idea of "Punch

Designing the Future

Through" very helpful when faced with a seemingly overwhelmingly difficult task that is just over the horizon,' he writes. 'The trick . . . is to prepare well and then to aim "past" the future event. Then imagine being in the future looking back at having already achieved a good outcome. Focus on the desired outcome, not the barriers.'[21]

Some wise person remarked that, 'the bend in the road is not the end of the road – unless you fail to make the curve.' Many people fail to negotiate the curves in the road, simply because they have given no forethought to the journey.

Of course, there are many things in life that we cannot predict – only God knows the beginning from the end. God spoke very clearly to the prophet Isaiah on this:

> *I am God, and there is no other; I am God, and there is none like me. I make known the end from the beginning, from ancient times, what is still to come. I say: My purpose will stand, and I will do all that I please. (Isaiah 46:9–10)*

God is writing *his* story throughout our history. However, God expects us to plan, where we can, to use imagination, faith and creativity to uncover his plans and bring them to fruition. That's what he meant when he told us to subdue the earth.[22]

In book one of this series, I mentioned Isaiah 43 and how the Lord calls on us to respond whenever we know he is about to do something new:

> *See, I am doing a new thing! Now it springs up; do you not perceive it? I am making a way in the desert and streams in the wasteland. (Isaiah 43:19)*

The word translated 'perceive' here can also be rendered as 'answer'. God is searching the earth for people who are prepared to be *pro*-active in his service. When he announces the 'new thing' he is doing, he expects us to answer the call, to start creating and shaping the future in line with his word. Lining up with a 'future word' requires strategic thought, planning and action.

If we are willing to apply our minds in a strategic way, identifying and responding to possible curves in the road ahead, we may find that we spend less time reacting to emergencies. We may find that we're able to exercise our faith in constructive ways, bringing the changes rather than just responding to them.

1. Charles Colson and Nancey Pearcey, *How Now Shall We Live?* (Tyndale House Publishers, 1999), p. 301
2. Quoted ibid., p. 301
3. Ibid., p. 302
4. Edward de Bono, *New Thinking for the New Millennium*, (Penguin Books, 2000), p. 48
5. Revelation 11:15
6. Revelation 7:9
7. Matthew 5–7
8. Quoted by John Maxwell, *The 21 Irrefutable Laws of Leadership* (Nelson, 1998), p. 192
9. Proverbs 29:18, King James Version
10. Proverbs 29:18, The Living Bible
11. Matthew 6:33, English Standard Version
12. Cf. John 14:31
13. Hebrews 12:1–2
14. Ephesians 2:20
15. Edward de Bono, *New Thinking for the New Millennium* (Penguin Books, 2000), p.109

Designing the Future   55

16. Howard G. Hendricks, *Color Outside the Lines* (Word Publishing, 1998), pp. 12–13
17. Edward de Bono, Op Cit., p. 109
18. Stephen Reid, *How to Think: Building Your Mental Muscle* (Pearson Education Limited, 2002), p. 179
19. Acts 21:13
20. Hebrews 11:1
21. Stephen Reid, ibid., p. 60
22. Genesis 1:28

4

Re-digging the Wells

It is almost unbearably hot. A prolonged drought is ravaging the already arid deserts of the Middle East.

In the midst of all the misery, one man has the power to bring at least a little relief to this parched landscape. He is called Isaac. He has inherited some wells; deep water holes that were first constructed by his father, a wealthy herdsman named Abraham.

These wells could water Isaac's flocks, and those of his many of his neighbours. Strangely, though, men from the surrounding cities of Philistia have blocked up the wells. They have covered them over, as if to hide them completely.

Isaac, though, refuses to be robbed of his inheritance. He uncovers the wells left him by his father, Abraham. In the process, he not only liberates a much-needed source of sustenance but he also recovers something even more valuable than water . . .

Living in the desert during a time of drought, you might expect that the Philistines of Genesis 26 were delighted to have a few more wells around the place. They weren't. Instead, they plugged up the wells of Abraham. Literally,

Re-digging the Wells

the passage says that they 'hid them from view' or 'kept them secret.'[1]

In those days, wells were much more than sources of water. They represented influence. In an agrarian society, to control the wells was to command the wealth. Water was the lifeline for animals and crops, and trading tended to happen near wells. What's more, the owners of the wells had a significant say in town planning, because whole villages and settlements sprang up around water holes.

So, masters of wells were influential people. The Philistines did not want Isaac to wield the kind of authority his father had known. So, they tried to conceal the wells. Isaac, however, refused to let the Philistines rob him of his inheritance of influence.

As we look back on two millennia of Christian history, we can see that the spiritual fathers of the church left us with a powerful legacy. In their time, they dug some deep spiritual wells. That's especially true in the nations of Western Europe.

In Acts 16, Paul planned to continue his travels in Asia Minor, going even further eastwards. The Holy Spirit closed that door and sent him westwards, into Europe. For centuries since then the history of global evangelism, church planting and world-changing outreach was the story of European Christianity. The world heard about Jesus because European Christians were willing to pray, sacrifice, preach and lay down their lives for the gospel. We could easily include many European names in the Hebrews 11 honour roll:

And what more shall I say? I do not have time to tell about [Luther, Wesley, Müller, Livingstone, Taylor, Studd and Carey], who through faith conquered kingdoms, administered justice, and gained what was

58 *The Pioneer Spirit*

promised; who shut the mouths of [spiritual] lions, quenched the fury of the flames, and escaped the edge of the sword; whose weakness was turned to strength; and who became powerful in [spiritual] battle and routed foreign armies.' (Hebrews 11:32–34 – with some European additions!)

As Christians, we are heirs to a great tradition of influence. Today, however, there are over 250,000 European cities, towns and villages that have no Christian church. Dr Yonggi Cho says, 'All over Europe, there are tombstones to a dead God ... they're called cathedrals.' *TIME* magazine has called Western Europe the least religious place on earth. So great is the spiritual need in the developed countries of Europe, that God is sending them apostles, prophets and evangelists from third world countries.

Taking Responsibility

In Europe and in other parts of the western world, the Philistines have hidden the wells of our influence; they have overrun us.

In the face of this, many church leaders have placed their hopes in the latest 'revival' to create the break-throughs they need. This is little more than an abdication of responsibility. If, in the midst of my own work, I am touched by revival in another church or nation, this does not absolve me of my obligation to seek God for vision at home. Or, to develop strategies that will carry the gospel to the lost.

Historically, the word 'revival' has generally been used to describe times when extraordinary numbers of people have come to Christ. Church historians speak of spiritual

Re-digging the Wells 59

'awakenings', in which there was a marked increase of interest in godly things across cities and nations. People were converted in huge numbers in a relatively short space of time.

Charles Finney was at the forefront of one such national awakening. He led over one million people to Christ, in the days before mass communications and media. Many know him now as the father of modern revival. Finney wrote extensively on revival. He always stressed that the true mark of revival is that unsaved people come to Christ.

For many Christians today, though, 'revival' means a season of unusual phenomena within the church. It signifies a time of extraordinary signs following the preaching of God's word, but has less to do with salvation. Revival has somehow come to be associated with the needs of the church rather than those of the outside world.

God most definitely *does* revive his church. He *does* breathe new life into tired bodies – and often in unexpected ways. For example, the Asuza Street revival in America saw an outbreak of Holy Spirit manifestations similar to those in the New Testament. Under the empowering of the Spirit, people prophesied and spoke in other languages, much as they did on the day of Pentecost.[2] Sick bodies were healed and miracles occurred.

At the time – in the first decade of the twentieth century – many professing Christians were stunned and even frightened by these strange events. Most of the established churches closed their doors to the peculiar working of God's Spirit. The church had come so far from its first-century roots, that it didn't recognize its own reflection in the mirror. Yet, many people were drawn to Christ and new churches sprang up around the world, boldly proclaiming that they were 'Pentecostal'.

More recently, the revival some have coined the

60 *The Pioneer Spirit*

'Toronto Blessing' saw unusual manifestations of the joy of the Lord. The so-called 'Pensacola Revival' saw thousands of people coming to Christ. Here, the Spirit of God moved to bring a deep sense of conviction of sin and the need for repentance.

Each of these contemporary events contained the true work of the Spirit of God. However, some people have tried to build institutions and systems of doctrine around these centres of experience. They've started treating the signposts as if they were the destination.

I was once given a very special alarm clock for my birthday. It was very high-tech for its time – it came complete with a built-in snooze function and radio. Every morning, the alarm would sound and my favourite music would fill the room. I could reach over, hit the snooze button, and give myself a few more minutes of slumber before getting up to face the world. The snooze alert was great, unless I abused it. On occasion, I'd whack 'snooze' just a couple of times too many and end up being late for an important appointment.

Revivals within the church are God's wake up call to his people. Revivals are our alarm clock, waking us to the needs of the world, and empowering us to meet those needs. Sadly, though, some Christians experience revival, hit the snooze control and go back to sleep. They enjoy their revival for a moment, but then miss their most important appointment, which is kingdom influence.

The mistake some people make with seasons of revival is not that they expect too little, but that they want too much. They want God to fulfil the Great Commission for them. God will never do for us what he has com-missioned and empowered *us* to do for him – to go into the world, preach the gospel and make disciples.

Nations will not be changed simply because churches enjoy seasons of unusual phenomena. Nations will not

Re-digging the Wells

necessarily be impacted because we have months of revival meetings inside our churches. Nations will be affected as Christians fulfil the Great Commission in their various spheres of life, in the energy of the Holy Spirit. Revival power comes to strengthen us for the task of world mission, not to *replace* that task.

The church was not destined just to have internal revival. It was built to reform cities and nations. Christians are not called just to receive inspiration; we are commissioned to have influence.

We must do more than look to the heavens for rain; we must dig the ground at our feet! We must uncover the wells left by our fathers.

The Philistines we must contend with are very different from the warriors of Isaac's time, but they're no less dangerous. We face the Philistines of humanism (which says, 'blessed are the godless'), materialism ('blessed are the soulless') and hedonism ('blessed are the thoughtless'). Then there are the Philistines of liberalism ('blessed are the lawless'), consumerism ('blessed are the limitless') and socialism ('blessed are the risk-less').

A century under these influences has, as far as Europe is concerned, covered over the wells left us by our fathers. They have robbed new generations of the incredible power of risk-taking, heroic Christian faith.

Yet, despite the opposition, there *are* people in Europe and in the West generally who are forming an Isaac offence-force. New pioneers *are* arising: Christians and ministry leaders who recognize the wells under their feet and have started to dig!

These leaders see the importance of creativity and strategic thinking, as well as spiritual renewal. They know that strategic thinking cannot take the place of God's power. All the planning in the world will lead only to dust and ashes, unless the Holy Spirit breathes upon

62 *The Pioneer Spirit*

it.[3] Yet, research and forward planning can help the church to identify where it most needs God's help, and where people are most open to the gospel. Strategic planning provides channels into society, through which revival power can flow.

All too often, we lose the long-term impact of revival in the church, simply because we've given no forethought as to where it might be leading us.

Building Your Strategic Muscle . . .

Strategic thinking is more a skill than an art. It can be learned, practised and developed.

'Strategic planning,' says media writer Viggo Sorgaard, 'is a continuous process of making risk-taking decisions.'[4] It simply involves a continuous process, a cycle, of thinking, planning, acting, then evaluating and back to thinking again. There are many skills available to help us think more strategically. Here are some examples that you might like to study further:

1. *Brainstorming*

It sounds like something that happens to you when you've seen one too many of those *Funniest Home Video* programmes. (You know, when your brain starts short-circuiting and thundering: 'I can't take this any more!')

In fact, brainstorming is one of the most effective tools for innovative thinking. It allows people to release their inherent creative abilities in a stream-of-consciousness, free flow of ideas.

Brainstorming is a technique to get your mind working and to get you out of thinking along predictable lines. The flow of electric current between the neurones of the brain tends to happen along established pathways. As we

Re-digging the Wells

experience different things, we develop habits of thinking. The brain likes to simplify complex experiences to make them more manageable. Over time, the brain will teach itself to respond to a certain stimulus in a predetermined way. Rather than come up with a new response every time, the brain will tend to fall back on predictable patterns it developed in the past. The more we experience a certain stimulus, the more entrenched our response to it is likely to be.

Most of the time, all this is a good thing. It means that the brain doesn't continually need to go back over old ground. If that happened, we'd never learn anything – we'd be experiencing things for the first time *every* time!

By developing patterns of thought, our brains help us keep things in perspective, giving us confidence and preventing us from being overwhelmed by our experiences. There can be a downside, however. If we're not careful, we can find ourselves in a rut and going through the motions. Brainstorming is one way of forcing our brains to take a different road now and again.

In a brainstorming session, leaders, designers or managers are able to throw ideas freely around the room, without fear of judgement or criticism. From those ideas, some of them wild and provocative, will come a short list of more viable and practical concepts.

If brainstorming is to work well in a team, a few basic ground rules must be applied. First, all criticism must be suspended. 'Criticism,' writes Howard Hendricks, 'is the mortician of the creative process.'[5] Our natural tendency, after years of analytical education, is to hesitate before sharing an idea, giving ourselves time to evaluate how others may react to it. While we're busy guarding ourselves against rejection, though, we may discard our best ideas.

We can also tend to judge other people's ideas too

The Pioneer Spirit

quickly. There are two fundamental patterns for thought. Some writers have called them 'convergent thinking' and 'divergent thinking'. Convergent thinking is all about focus. It's about converging on an answer; narrowing the options down as quickly as possible. Divergent thinking, however, likes to remain open for as long as possible. It can appear very vague, as it seeks to explore many creative alternatives.

Each one of us will tend to be more one or the other, though we will express characteristics from both categories at different times. Some of us want to get to a resolution of the problem as quickly as possible. Others want to hang loose and remain flexible. It can be difficult for strongly convergent thinkers to relate well to very divergent thinkers.

In terms of our education, I think, most of us are taught to be convergent thinkers. We're encouraged to get from A to B in the shortest possible time, with the least expenditure of energy. Sadly, that sometimes cuts us off from some exciting possibilities. Sometimes, it is better for us to suspend judgement until we have had the chance to explore the options.

Picture a funnel: the kind you use to pour petrol into a lawnmower, for example. One end is wide and open; the other is closed and focussed. The larger end might represent divergent thinking, the narrower end convergent thinking. It is a healthy exercise for 'wide end' thinkers to learn to get to the point now and again! But it's also important that 'narrow end' thinkers develop the capacity to suspend judgement, giving an idea time to germinate before they rush to find a conclusion.

That's the beauty of brainstorming and other techniques like it. They encourage divergent thinking in a world that constantly wants to rush toward the narrow end of the funnel. So, in a brainstorming session, people

Re-digging the Wells

should avoid saying things like, 'That's silly' or, 'You know that'll never work.' Judging the ideas comes later; brainstorming only works when people are released to be as innovative and daring as possible.

Ideas can always be toned down a little, but they can't be pumped up. So, a second guiding principle is that the wilder the ideas, the better. Risk-taking is a fundamental part of all creative thinking, so people must be willing to take a shot. They must be encouraged to let go with the really courageous ideas that might otherwise stay lurking in the recesses of their minds.

People should be encouraged to do a little mental 'hitchhiking' too. Sometimes, an idea suggested by one person, gives rise to other associations and people should be invited to follow these through. Of course, if you're leading one of these sessions you need to allow for this, without letting everyone just focus on one idea, so that the session gets bogged down. Brainstorming relies on the fact that you're *not* developing all the parts of one idea – no matter how good it is – until the session is ended. Brainstorming is like word association: it needs a momentum to develop, as people become more and more open.

Finally, it is important to appoint someone in the group to note down the ideas – all of them – so that they can be circulated for evaluation later. Of course, you may want to flesh out some of the ideas as soon as the brainstorming session is over. Usually, though, it's better to give people time to rest and reflect before you go on. At least give them a coffee break before proceeding.

A good brainstorming session might last for just twenty minutes. That's long enough for people to get into the exercise, yet short enough to stave off mental exhaustion! The creative process can really tax your energy levels.

2. Future-projecting

This process has also been called 'long-jumping'. It's a technique that allows you to think about the future by taking a mental jump from the present. When athletes compete in the long jump, they take a few steps back before projecting themselves forward. How do we apply this to mental exercise?

Future-projecting begins with identifying an aspect of the future you would like to focus on, and a time frame you would like to project to. For example, you might ask the question, 'I wonder what a local church will be like in the year 2020?' In that one sentence, you have set both the subject matter and the date.

Now, you must take three steps back. Pick three times in history to go back to, trying to spread them out so that you have a feeling of change over time. For example, you might try using the dates AD 100, AD 1600 and today. Use your imagination and what you know of history to describe what churches were like at each of those times.

Now you are ready to launch yourself into the future. Take the date you chose in your question – 2020 – and have some fun dreaming about what church might be like then. Write down any ideas that come to your mind, using your knowledge of human nature, technological developments, and trends in society. You don't need to be a scholar to do this – it should be fun.

The question now is this: how do you need to respond in the present to the vision you have of the future? Are there things in that vision that you would like to avoid and, if so, how can you do this? Are there things you would like to develop and work towards? What action do you need to take now to bring those results about? The answers to these questions will drive the innovative process. Remember that strategic thinking is about working backwards from the desired goal.

Re-digging the Wells

3. Objection-countering

This is a great technique for predicting likely opposition to a new idea and for developing plans to defuse problems. As the name suggests, it involves making a list of objections people might have to a strategy or vision. You may not agree with these objections; you're simply making a list of what people might say. Try to do it as rapidly as possible, to keep your creative juices flowing.

Once you have a reasonably sized list, go through it and begin to identify recurring themes. For example, if you're dealing with a new project, some of the objections might relate to cost. At the same time, cross off any objections that everyone agrees are highly unlikely and not worth worrying about.

Now, ask yourself some honest questions. Is there any truth in these objections? How can we set this programme in motion so that we anticipate these questions? How can we take the sting out of them by preparing ourselves in advance?

This process has been very helpful to businesses that want to launch a new product or service. Church leaders have also found it helpful in preparing people for the challenges of Christian living in a secularized world. Some churches, for example, have used objection-countering to prepare young people for life in university or college. Many students struggle to retain their faith in the face of the secular–humanist agenda of most modern universities. Objection-countering helps them identify some of the likely points of tension they'll face, and it gives them an opportunity to prepare responses in advance.

This technique can be invaluable for parents too, as we try to help our kids anticipate the hurdles they will face in life.

Strategic thinking always strives to be ahead of the game.

68   *The Pioneer Spirit*

4. Mind-mapping

This is one of my personal favourites. I love working with words, but sometimes my old architecture training kicks in and I find that I can work through concepts better with pictures. I think we all enjoy dragging out the fat crayons from time to time and releasing the frustrated Picasso inside of us.

Mind-mapping sounds like some kind of new age gimmick for aura-reading. Actually, it's a mechanism for drawing links between ideas or needs in a process. It's a great way of developing an overview of a situation.

The easiest way to go about this is to draw an oval shape in the centre of a page. Write in the oval the name of the project that you're working on or the need that you're trying to meet. Then draw a series of other ovals around the central one, with each representing one aspect of the overall problem. Connect these to the centre oval with lines. Now you have a central heading and a series of sub-headings.

Then, take each of the outer ovals and draw branches from them. Write on each branch a word or sentence that describes some key aspect of this part of the problem or project.

An illustration might help here. Before I wrote this book, I drew up a mind-map on my notebook computer, using a piece of software designed for that purpose. My central oval featured the words 'The Pioneer Spirit'. That was the definition of the project. From there, I draw other ovals; some of them featuring the chapter titles and others dealing with practical issues like size, cover art and so on. Then, each chapter heading was given a series of branches. Each branch dealt with a key point I wanted to raise in that chapter. I could also add projected time deadlines for the completion of each chapter.

Often, when I sat down to write, I would look back at

Re-digging the Wells 69

that picture. Of course, I was able to change it along the way as new things found their way into the book idea. However, having the picture in front of me has helped me to see the end from the beginning, so that I'm always aware of where I'm going. I use the same process in preparing articles and sermons.

We use mind-mapping in our TV production meetings, too. It's a great way to write up an agenda, because it allows you to add connected ideas without using words alone. And it's a lot more interesting to look at than a list written down the page!

5. Time-lines
The art of strategic thinking, remember, is to identify a preferred future and then develop practical steps that will take you there. The time-line technique is one tool that's used a great deal by project managers and strategic thinkers of all kinds.

Time-lining, like mind-mapping, starts with specifying your end target. Perhaps you have an event to plan. Draw a long line on a piece of paper and mark down at the end of the line the date of your event. The start of the line represents the present. Now, take a second piece of paper and brainstorm about all the tasks you will need to complete before the event. Then, make a more concrete list based on your brainstorm ideas.

The next step is simply to take the tasks and place them along your time-line, between the present and the event date. But don't work in forward motion – go backwards from just before the event itself. Specify a date for each task. Those dates will become your progressive deadlines. You can only reach the big deadline – the event date – by going through all the smaller ones. Usually, the days and weeks immediately before the event will be the most crowded, but you must try to spread things out as much as possible.

70   *The Pioneer Spirit*

Keep that time-line with you, either in your diary or notebook or on your computer. It will be your guide in managing time, resources and people. There are computer programs for constructing time-lines and most personal planner systems – Day Timer and Filofax, for example – have project-management attachments.

It's a good idea, at the beginning of each year, to develop time-lines for all of your major projects, responsibilities or goals. I've found that to be invaluable when it comes to managing a number of projects – and people – at once. You can always expect the unexpected, but good preparation can leave you with enough time and energy to deal with life's little twists.

6. *Romancing and plussing*

Romancing means taking an existing idea or project and tweaking it; adding some special touch to it. Walt Disney, one of the most innovative minds of the last century, romanced the amusement park and created a whole new thing: the theme park.

With any great idea, there is always a unique factor: something singular that is different and fresh, that approaches a familiar situation in a whole new way. Romancing an idea involves identifying the unique factor within it. Ask yourself or your team: What unique thing does our vision or project actually add to the world? How does it make the world a better place? How does it extend the Kingdom of God into new areas? Once you have identified the unique factor, develop it. Ask: What good idea have we – or other people – already put into practice that can be romanced to create something even better?

From time to time, even with well-established projects, it's a good idea to search for the unique factor all over again. (Sometimes, the unique factor manages to get buried under all kinds of administrative rubble!) Then,

Re-digging the Wells

imagine that you were starting from scratch, with nothing more than that one special idea. What would you build this time? How would that be different from what you have in place now? In the light of that, how can you improve what you have now?

Plussing means playing with an idea or project so that you are always improving on it and adapting it to meet the need. It means never settling for the status quo, even when you've already developed a truly great project, ministry or idea.

The key to leadership in any field is to stay at or near the front by constantly adding innovation and improvement. That can be very hard work. Our human nature would rather have us sitting back and enjoying the fruits of our success. The pioneer spirit, however, demands that we keep boldly going where we've never gone before – and taking others along for the ride.

Other processes can help you become more strategic in your planning – for example, role-playing and Edward de Bono's 'Thinking Hats' process. There are specialist books on this sort of thing and they're well worth a look, especially if you want to develop your strategic muscle.

Techniques like these can be a lot of fun, and that's important when you're trying to be creative. Jesus said that we must become like children if we are to inherit God's kingdom.[6] If we're going to be inventive in a kingdom way, we must learn to create as children do – with an attitude of playfulness. For children, having fun is a vital part of the process of producing something: it's not just something to be enjoyed once the job is done. Children explore, prod, experiment and develop – and they take pleasure from their work. Their best toys double as tools.

The thinking tools described above should be used in fun ways, so that we can achieve a serious result. They

72 *The Pioneer Spirit*

are proven creative techniques that will help us to explore challenges and problems from unexpected angles. They can lift us out of our comfort zones so that we see things from a fresh vantage point.

Used well, these techniques will release us from the tyranny of the moment, so that our thinking soars in the freedom of future-mindedness. They will inspire the playful and ever curious pioneer within us!

1. Genesis 26:15
2. See Acts 2
3. Psalm 127:1 and Zechariah 4:6
4. Viggo Sorgaard, *Media in Church and Mission: Communicating the Gospel* (William Carey Library, 1993), p. 225
5. Howard Hendricks, Op Cit., p. 110
6. Mark 10:15

5

You Are That Road Runner!

It is spring in Australia, the year, 2000. For two weeks, Sydney has become, in the eyes of the world, the city of champions.

The world's vast media machine has swung into action, focussing hearts and minds around the planet on the extraordinary exploits of some very special young people.

The city is infused with the spirit of youthful enthusiasm, as world-class athletes thrill packed stadiums with their feats of skill, endurance and sheer tenacity. The word 'champion' is everywhere: it is featured in every newspaper and magazine and on every TV newscast.

This is truly a special Olympic gathering: special because of the turning of a millennium and because these are truly the 'friendly games'. Here, old champions are honoured and new ones are born. Muhammad Ali looks on as Cathy Freeman competes.

For every competitor, the stakes are high and the potential rewards well worth the four years spent in arduous preparation. Young boys and girls around the planet follow the exploits of these larger-than-life heroes, hatching their own dreams of future glory as champions of the world.

The Pioneer Spirit

The word 'champion' is used so often these days that repetition can easily dull our minds to its real meaning.

A real champion is several things. For one, he or she is someone who excels. Champions stand head and shoulders above their peers. A champion is also someone who competes on behalf of others, representing a group, a city, or a nation in sport or – as the word was often used of old – in war. I think, though, that the bottom line is this: *a champion is someone who refuses to be ignored!*

None of us likes being ignored. I don't know anybody who enjoys feeling unappreciated. Married men and women experience great angst if they are overlooked by their partners. Friendships break up when people stop paying attention to one another. Children who are long neglected by their parents, starved of emotional nurturing, grow up with dysfunctional emotions and stunted self-esteem.

Somewhere deep in the psyche of every human being, there lies a drive to be appreciated and noticed, a yearning to have significance for other people. We need to have influence on others – it's in our wiring.

I remember the first time I saw Michael Jordan play basketball. What an athlete! He could run the length of the court in just a few emu-like strides. He leapt like a kangaroo on steroids – and turned in mid-air, so that he seemed to be walking on air.

Watching Michael at work, I got a bit carried away. For a while, it wasn't Jordan I was watching – it was me, Air Fletcher. It was me out there slam-dunking the opposition, smiling for the cameras and drinking in the adoration of the crowd. For a very short time, I exchanged places with an athletic genius, if only inside my own head.

We all love heroes because we like to identify with them. We love to imagine what it would be like to live in

You Are That Road-Runner!

their shoes. Deep within us is a drive to experience a heroic, larger-than-life existence. We long to be applauded.

When a person becomes a Christian, they come into a whole new level of opportunity for influence. The apostle Paul was doubtless one of the most influential men in history. As we've already noted, he was one of the first Christian leaders to take the good news of Christ to the non-Jewish nations. He was definitely the first to establish a beachhead for the gospel in Western Europe.

As one scholar noted, 'When Paul began his ministry a gentile was an oddity in the church. Before his death, the eastern part of the Roman Empire had in large measure heard the gospel message.'[1]

Paul gave us thirteen of the twenty-seven books of the New Testament, and had more of an impact on the long-term formation of the church than any other individual, aside from Jesus. It was Paul who established once and for all that a man cannot be justified before God by virtue of his good works – that only faith in Christ can save him. When Luther made his courageous stand before the Council at Worms, it was Paul who provided the platform. Paul inspired the Reformation. Fifteen hundred years after they had laid his body in the ground, he was still changing the world!

Fundamental to Paul's preaching and writing is the idea that followers of Christ are called to make a deep impression on the world in which they live. To the Roman believers, he said this:

> *Do not conform any longer to the pattern of this world, but be transformed by the renewing of your mind. Then you will be able to test and approve what God's will is – his good, pleasing and perfect will. (Romans 12:2)*

76   *The Pioneer Spirit*

He challenged them to exercise more influence over their culture than it did over them. And so it is throughout all of his letters: Christians are born (again) for influence. In his second letter to the Corinthians, Paul gave us another insight into this calling:

We, however, will not boast beyond proper limits, but will confine our boasting to the field God has assigned to us, a field that reaches even to you. (2 Corinthians 10:13)

In the passage surrounding this verse, Paul was defending his right to speak with the authority of a pioneer apostle. He'd played a big part in bringing the gospel to these people and therefore felt that he had the right to speak to their spiritual condition. They were, he said, a part of the 'field' of responsibility that God had entrusted to him as a pioneer leader.

Paul's choice of words in this verse is interesting, because the word translated 'field' is a Greek one that means 'a limited sphere' or 'a measured zone'. According to Paul, God had marked out a sphere of influence for his life, an area in which he was called to produce change for the Kingdom of God. The church at Corinth lay within that sphere.

The apostles of old were not the only ones to whom God gave a sphere of influence. *Every Christian* has a God-given zone in which they can produce change. That's what Paul referred to when he said:

For we are God's workmanship, created in Christ Jesus to do good works, which God prepared in advance for us to do. (Ephesians 2:10)

We all have acquaintances, friends, family members and work colleagues on whom we can make an impression

You Are That Road-Runner! 77

for Christ. We all have careers, hobbies and other activities that can become conduits for the spread of the good news. We all live in some apartment building, neighbourhood or community where we can be the salt of the earth, preserving righteousness, and flavouring our world so that it pleases God.

Our TV producer, Tina Meyer, was once part of a unit that was filming a soap opera. In the initial team-building exercise, every member was asked to describe their greatest ambition in life. Tina's response was simply this: 'I want to make a difference.' That's the bottom-line calling of *every* Christian – to change the way things are done on God's earth. We don't do that by coercing people, but by leading winsome lives and, in the process, making our faith attractive to people.

If you're a team sports fan, you'll be very familiar with the idea of a zone of play. There are defensive zones and offensive zones. Players are assigned zones based on their gifts and their training. Coaches are always telling players to get in their zone. The team can only progress when every player performs well within his or her sphere of influence. It's the same with the Kingdom of God.

God has a zone of influence for your life. Your real success in life will occur within that sphere. Paul saw great results within his zone of influence. He didn't need to labour in someone else's field, because there was enough to do in his own:

What, after all, is Apollos? And what is Paul? Only servants, through whom you came to believe – as the Lord has assigned to each his task. I planted the seed, Apollos watered it, but God made it grow. So neither he who plants nor he who waters is anything, but only God, who makes things grow. (1 Corinthians 3:5–7)

78 *The Pioneer Spirit*

Paul knew where his zone ended and other men's started. He didn't feel the need to compete with contemporaries like Apollos. He'd learned to recognize and appreciate his own field of ministry.

God's sphere of influence for your life is bigger than you think. It is not marked out by some tiny circle drawn close to your feet. It is so big that you will spend the rest of your days trying to fill it! Your zone of influence is so large that it will demand more than the investment of your small change or your spare time. It will require that you give your entire life to it!

If you were to really see how much influence God wants *you* to have, you would never again aspire to be anyone else. You'd be too excited about your own prospects and far too caught up walking toward your own promise. Paul knew what that was like, which is why he could write these words to the Ephesians:

> *God can do anything, you know – far more than you could ever imagine or guess or request in your wildest dreams! He does it by . . . working within us.* (Ephesians 3:20, The Message)

When you became a Christian, you were grafted into a great tree of influence that has spread its branches through every generation and nation on earth.

Small Degrees of Power – Large Amounts of Influence

Throughout history, as today, pioneer leaders are hungry for influence – they pursue it with zest. True godly pioneers are not sidetracked by status, or by offers of title or position, because their eyes are fastened on influence.

You Are That Road-Runner! 79

One of the most significant marks of the ministry of Paul was that he rarely took the path others might have chosen for him. Great pioneers seldom make good career moves!

He was born in Tarsus, which is now part of Turkey, around AD 15 and quite possibly educated in the University of Tarsus. His profession: tent-maker. For a while, he spent his time throwing Christians into prison. He made sure that he was present when the evangelist Stephen was stoned to death; he was witness to the first Christian martyrdom.[2]

Just as he was building a fine career as a zealous Pharisee, a defender of the Law, he threw it all away to join the enemy! Around AD 34, he had a vision of the risen Christ.[3] This experience changed his life – and the history of the world. For over a decade, Paul served as part of a local church at Antioch. Somewhere in that time, he became one of its leaders. This was a prestigious and resourceful church, which sent many evangelists into new areas. It was in Antioch that believers were first called 'Christians'. This church had vision and influence. I suppose that if they had *Hillsong* conferences in those days, they were holding them at Antioch.

Before Paul could enjoy his status, though, God uprooted him and sent him out on a missionary journey with fellow preacher, Barnabas. This trip took them to Cyprus and Galatia and lasted from AD 46 to 48. Paul went from prominence in one of the world's leading churches, to obscurity, planting churches in places where the gospel was not even known. Again, it was not an upward step, career-wise.

In AD 48, Barnabas presented Paul to the apostles in Jerusalem. Once, these men regarded Paul as their fiercest foe. Now, though, he had some points on the board. His ministry was proof of his Christian conversion

80 *The Pioneer Spirit*

and call. I suppose Paul might have been comfortable staying with the apostles in Jerusalem. It was, after all, the centre of the Jewish world – and, at that time, the centre of the Christian one, too. Again, though, God moved him on.

He stepped away from mixing with *the* leaders of the church, the friends of Christ, to devote his life to people who'd never heard about Jesus at all. From AD 49 to 57, he established the first Christian churches in Asia Minor and the Balkans, and laid the groundwork for Christian expansion in the West. These were incredibly productive years, with churches planted and leaders equipped and set in place. Surely now Paul would get to enjoy the fruits of his labours.

No. In AD 59, Paul made one more pioneering journey. It started in Jerusalem, where he was seized by an angry mob, and ended in Rome, where he was imprisoned. He might have avoided arrest, had he not been so keen to preach at his own trial![4] He stayed under house arrest there for two years, during which time he wrote some of his most potent letters. Finally, around AD 61 or 62, he was martyred for his faith.

Now, if you'd been around at the time, you might be excused for thinking that this was a sorry end to what could have been a brilliant career. Paul, the one who could dazzle a crowd with his oratory, and impress philosophers with his razor-sharp debating skills; Paul, who had the authority to challenge even the great apostle Peter on matters of doctrine; Paul, who could heal the sick and raise the dead, surely, he could have done better than this.

All the way along, Paul made what some people would consider terrible career moves. He constantly walked away from opportunities to settle back, build a power base and protect his own position.

You Are That Road-Runner! 81

Early in his ministry, it would have been easy for Paul to pack his duffle bag and trot off to Rome. This was, after all, the New York of its time, the Big Apple. If you could make it there, you could make it anywhere. From Rome, Paul could have made a real name for himself. He could have come into some serious influence and found his name plastered all over the glossy Christian magazines. Some might have seen this as a logical progression for a gifted guy like Paul, yet he refused to be drawn. He was not enamoured with human concepts of promotion, or with moving up the corporate ladder. He only responded to moves based on a call.

It is sad to see how some believers are motivated by nothing more than their next step up the career ladder, or by the next status symbol they can buy. Their decisions are based on achieving a success that's defined by comfort, celebrity and title or by the size of their stock portfolio. Many Christians settle for small degrees of power, when God has destined them for large amounts of influence. Some of them are responding out of fear, rather than faith.

In the 1970s, futurist Alvin Toffler foresaw a 'roaring current of change' that would leave many people feeling disoriented and alone. His prescient words are fulfilled in our time. Looking at the seemingly overwhelming changes confronting them, many Christians become legalistic. That is, they start hiding behind man-made rules and traditions rather than engaging the world around them with compassion and hope.

Others become jingoistic – they would rather stand behind comfortable clichés than become real and vulnerable with a hurting world. Still others turn to institutions for their sense of support. They start jockeying for position in business or church life, rather than working to change the wider world.

82   *The Pioneer Spirit*

Sadly, some church leaders are concerned more with career promotion within their denominational structures than with bringing about change in the world. When this happens to us, we shift our focus away from risk-taking faith to the kind of middle management we see in corporate structures. There's nothing wrong with good management. But managers do not create breakthroughs – pioneer visionaries do that!

Danger: Ziklag Ahead!

Aside from Jesus, no biblical king was greater than Israel's David. From humble beginnings, David rose to become a leader who made Israel not only a strong and prosperous nation, but also a nation that loved God and served his purposes.

Despite his obscure origins and his sometimes-wavering faith, David was given a great epitaph in Scripture. He was called a man after God's own heart.[5] He was a man God could relate to! What was it that marked David out for this kind of honour?

When you study the life of David, one quality stands out more than most – his passion. He was passionate in war. Facing Goliath's nine-foot frame, he declared, 'Who is this uncircumcised Philistine, that he should defy the armies of the living God?'[6] (Rough translation: 'Just who does this great, hairy son-of-a-motherless-goat think he is?')

David was passionate in worship, too. When he danced before the ark of the Lord, celebrating its return to Israel, he did it with so much energy that his wife accused him of making a public exhibition of himself before his female subjects. His response was typically blunt:

You Are That Road-Runner! 83

I will celebrate before the LORD. I will become even more undignified than this, and I will be humiliated in my own eyes. But by these slave girls you spoke of, I will be held in honour. (2 Samuel 6:21–22)

David was also ardent in love. Because he couldn't discipline that particular kind of passion, he found himself in big trouble with God. Thankfully, he was just as earnest when it came to repenting and turning his life back to God.[7] Although the damage had been done, God kept his promise to David, allowing his son to succeed him on the throne.

David's life was one of zeal, from start to finish. Whether he was slaying the lions and bears he met as a shepherd-boy, or standing up to a giant who defied his God, David knew how to express passion for a righteous cause. Yet, there was a time when David grew weary of being maligned, misunderstood and under-appreciated in Saul's Israel. For a while he left behind the land of his inheritance and took up residence in a city of the Philistines called Ziklag.[8]

Perhaps he thought that here, finally, he would find some respect. The Philistines talked of his exploits; they even feared him. Perhaps he thought he might find security and a sense of calm after the turbulent years spent as a fugitive from Saul. Perhaps he thought Ziklag would be the place where God would justify his cause and bring him into his promised destiny.

He may have had great hopes going into Ziklag, but the only things David found there were misery, loss and despair. One day, some enemies raided the town while he and his men were out crusading. That day, David lost his wives, his children and the loyalty of his fighting men. So great was the pain of his warriors that, at one point, they talked of stoning him.[9]

84 *The Pioneer Spirit*

It's been said that Satan doesn't want much from you – he only wants your treasure, your children and your inheritance. That's true. What else would you expect from someone whose sole pleasure is to steal, kill and destroy?[10]

Ziklag was not where God wanted David to be. It was a city of compromise: a place of refuge without revelation. David had received no instruction from the Lord telling him to go there. In the end, God had to mount a rescue operation to get David out of a situation in which he should never have placed himself to begin with.

Rescue operations always cost time, effort and valuable resources; they divert creative reserves away from one objective toward another. David and his men had to fight to win back what they already owned! They spent time and energy making up lost ground, when they could have been taking over new territory. Instead of calling the shots, they had to play catch-up football. Rather than pioneering new things, they struggled just to maintain the status quo. They owed all this to Ziklag.

Rescue operations also cost you passion. David and his men wept, the Bible says, until they had no more strength to weep.[11] Imagine what good they might have done with all that passion: what battles they could have fought in God's name; what enemy ground they could have taken for his cause. Battles went unfought because of Ziklag; enemies were left unconquered because of Ziklag; opportunities for expansion went unrealized because of Ziklag; an awesome fighting force almost fell apart, all because of Ziklag.

As a Christian, you are a product not of your past but of God's promise for your future. God's promise is a postcard of your future, with a caption that says, 'I wish you were here.' It's a picture of how tomorrow will look if you obey God's call.

God's promises are certain, because of what Jesus has done for us.

You Are That Road-Runner! 85

For no matter how many promises God has made, they are 'Yes' in Christ. (2 Corinthians 1:20)

Nothing can rob me of my destiny in God, provided I stay in Christ – under his covering and in his will.

The promises of God are also worth waiting for. In the Bible, winners – those who received God's promise for their future – always knew how to wait, while losers grew impatient and blew their chances. There are many examples of people who couldn't wait for the promise. Adam couldn't wait for understanding. Esau was impatient for his birthright. Saul was itching to go to battle and tried to play prophet as well as king. The prodigal son couldn't wait for his father to die – he wanted his inheritance *now*! Judas Iscariot refused to wait for the benefits of Jesus' kingdom – he wanted his piece of the action right away.

Then there are the faithful who didn't mind the wait, though it was very uncomfortable at times. Abram (finally) learned to wait for a son. Joseph learned to wait for the fulfilment of his dream. Moses learned that he couldn't hurry Israel's deliverance. Caleb waited until old age to claim his inheritance in Canaan. Daniel was willing to pray for Israel's deliverance, knowing that he'd never live to see it. Nehemiah was willing to fight with one hand, while he built Jerusalem's walls with the other.

Patience makes time the servant of God. Compromise makes God the servant of time. Patience is motivated by faith that says, 'It will happen, so I can wait.' Compromise is a product of fear and doubt: 'It may not happen, so I'll have to help it along.' Patience keeps us behind God where faith grows. Compromise tries to move us ahead of God where insecurity looms large.

I have a friend in La Pas, the capital of Bolivia. His name is Alberto Salcedo Penaloza and he is the leader of

86 *The Pioneer Spirit*

an exciting, growing church. In 1985, Pastor Alberto's church had just one hundred and fifty people in it. Today, it numbers over twenty thousand – and it's still growing! Across the nation, another twenty thousand people belong to other churches in his network. These churches own a group of TV stations and they control several radio stations. They have influence.

A little while back, the authorities in his city came to see Pastor Alberto. They told him they liked what he stood for and the way he led his people. They asked if he would be prepared to serve as mayor of the city. That's quite an opportunity for a pastor, especially one who wants to impact a nation!

Now, I can imagine that taking a church from one hundred and fifty people to over twenty thousand in just sixteen years would be a tiring task. Working through all the issues involved with leading people beyond where they've ever been, or ever dreamed of going, is a very draining experience. Pastor Alberto might have seen the city's offer as the sure road to the kind of influence for which he was called. God had been preparing him for national leadership; perhaps this would be God's door into that inheritance.

Alberto, however, saw things differently. He recognized the offer for what it was – a Ziklag opportunity. If he became mayor, he would be taking refuge in what was, for him at least, a city of compromise. 'I will help you find the right candidate,' he told the councillors. 'I will pray for God's guidance, too. But being a mayor is not my calling. God commissioned me to build a great church – and that's what I will go on doing, by God's grace.'

When we throw off impatience for the promises God has made, our zeal is re-fired. Passion is revived when we abandon the call to settle for Ziklag, the city of

You are that Road Runner!

I confess! I'm the sort of person that learns a great deal watching Warner Brothers cartoons. Like a lot of people, I grew up watching the escapades of Bugs ('that wascally wabbit'), Daffy ('Duck Dodgers'), Porky ('bedeer, bedeer, that's all folks . . . ') and all their mates. Maybe you're just like me – you still laugh, though you've seen them all a thousand times.

Of all the cartoon characters to come out of the Warner Brothers stable of stars, one of my all-time favourites has to be the Road Runner. Since I've been living in Europe, I've come to appreciate Road Runner cartoons even more – they're about the only cartoons the Europeans don't dub. They've managed to get Bugs to speak German. They've even got Daffy speaking Swedish. But what can they do with the Road Runner? Who wants to translate 'bip bip'?! Sure, the French would love to have 'le bip, le bip', but it's just not the same, is it?

The other reason I like Road Runner is that he just can't be beaten. No matter what his mortal enemy, the ravenous Coyote, throws at him, Road Runner always escapes unscathed. It might be the ACME jet shoes, the ACME hand-grenade tennis balls, or an ACME cannon. Sometimes, it's the Back-Mounted Rocket-Driven Propulsion Unit – built by, you guessed it, ACME. It doesn't matter what is the weapon-of-the-day, Road Runner will always walk away.

Sometimes, it's almost as if Road Runner lives on a different plane, that he inhabits a higher state of being

88 *The Pioneer Spirit*

than Coyote. Remember this scene? Coyote paints a picture of a highway on a solid brick wall. The scene shows the road receding into the distance, over the hills and far away. Having finished his masterpiece of perspective painting, Coyote takes cover behind a rock and waits for Road Runner to crash into the wall.

What happens next? Road Runner comes speeding down the road, burning up the tarmac and, without missing a beat, he just runs straight into that picture, as if it was real. You watch him make his escape along that painted highway, receding into the distance, over the hills and far away.

Coyote thinks to himself, something wonderful is happening here! He tries the same trick. But when he launches himself full throttle at the wall, POW, it's Coyote paste. No matter what weapons the Coyote uses, our little feathered hero always lives to tell the tale. The best-laid plans backfire on the hapless hound!

It may surprise you to know that, according to the Bible, you are that Road Runner! Now, I can almost hear some of you. 'Oh yeah, and where's that in the Bible?' you say. 'I'd like a text for that, if you don't mind!' OK. I'm happy to oblige:

> 'No weapon forged against you will prevail, and you will refute every tongue that accuses you. This is the heritage of the servants of the LORD, and this is their vindication from me,' declares the LORD. (Isaiah 54:17)

That word 'weapon' can actually be translated as 'apparatus' or 'machine'. You, too, have an enemy. Like Coyote, he enjoys creating all kinds of devious machines for your destruction. You, however, will always walk away without harm, because that is your right as a child of God. When the enemy puts stone walls in front of you, God paints a way of escape and turns the attack into blessing:

You Are That Road-Runner! 89

> *And God is faithful; he will not let you be tempted beyond what you can bear. But when you are tempted, he will also provide a way out so that you can stand up under it. (1 Corinthians 10:13)*

The whole world may be going to the dogs – or Coyotes – around you, but you will stay under the cover of God's glory and favour:

> *See, darkness covers the earth and thick darkness is over the peoples, but the LORD rises upon you and his glory appears over you. (Isaiah 60:2)*

Revivalists of old wrote about the 'weight of glory' that rests upon every Christian. Now that you are in Christ, there is an added dimension to your life. You live in this world, but you are not made of the same stuff. You are here, but you're not all here. The lights are on . . . but this is not your home. Like the Road Runner, there are times when you will walk through otherwise deadly situations, without so much as a scratch.

Perhaps the saddest thing in the world is to watch as some Christians remove the cloak of God's glory from their lives. Through compromise and apathetic, undisciplined living, they descend from their lofty place of safety, choosing to walk at the same level as Coyote. Now, they're living in the same dimension as their enemy. Suddenly, arrows that once bounced off them are piercing them through. When the enemy places a stone barrier before them, they no longer have the faith to run straight through it. They've become blind to God's way of escape.

If you ask some Christians about their aspirations, they'll respond in exactly the same way as their unsaved friends. 'I want to be happy,' they'll say. 'I want to be

90   *The Pioneer Spirit*

healthy. I want to have a nice career and a good life.'

There's nothing wrong with those goals, except that, for a Christian, they're not big enough! Friend, Jesus called you for much more than that. You've been set apart to change the world![12] And when you've finished transforming this one, you get to rule the next.[13]

Jesus came to give us life to the max.[14] Our lives in him should be lived at a higher level – for loftier purposes and with greater power – than the kind of humdrum, day-to-day human existence we see all around us. We don't live for just the next party, the next vacation, or the next promotion. We are alive, at this particular point in history, for a great purpose, to fill a large sphere of influence given to us by God himself.

Pioneers of faith refuse to settle for status, position, titles or power when they can have real influence under the cover of God's glory.

1. Charles F. Pfeiffer, *Baker's Bible Atlas* (Baker Book House, 1963, 1974), p. 215
2. Acts 8:1
3. See Acts 22
4. Cf. Acts 21:13 and 25:25
5. 1 Samuel 13:14
6. 1 Samuel 17:26
7. See Psalm 51
8. 1 Samuel 27:1–7
9. 1 Samuel 30:1–6
10. John 10:10
11. 1 Samuel 30:4
12. Matthew 5:17
13. Revelation 22:3–5
14. John 10:10

6

Pioneer Alliances

Martha Williamson is a young TV writer and producer. She has come out of college to make her mark in Hollywood.

One day, CBS-TV approaches Martha with an offer. They want her to be the executive producer of a new show, a programme about angels.

Studio polls have revealed that 70 per cent of Americans share a belief in angels, and the network wants to tap into this.

Martha agrees to look at the programme, but what she sees fails to impress. Martha is a committed Christian. The studio's concept depicts angels as down-to-earth, pragmatic good-guys, who sometimes bend God's rules in order to get his work done here on earth. God, on the other hand, is depicted as a slightly dim-witted boss who doesn't know how things are done in the 'real world'.

Martha politely turns down the studio offer. Shortly afterwards, when she's about to accept a much more lucrative job, God speaks to her in a very clear way. The Lord tells her to take the job. Instead of trashing the concept, she must reform it, from the inside.

Eventually, through Martha's efforts and commitment,

91

92 *The Pioneer Spirit*

the programme is totally revamped and given a new name: Touched by an Angel.

Today, *Touched by an Angel* has an audience of millions of people in America and many more around the world. No, it is not a Billy Graham crusade or a Benny Hinn healing service, but it *is* having an influence for the gospel. It is making people think again about their place under God, and how he might want to interact with them. It is making them look at their lives in the light of eternity.

Martha took on an idea that was not all it could be, a concept with which she was not happy. She didn't trash it, she redeemed it, turning it around and making it something that could honour God. True pioneers, like Martha, know how to stand on the shoulders of others, to build on – or redeem – what others are doing.

At the beginning of this book, I quoted something written by the apostle Paul:

> *I have trailblazed a preaching of the Message of Jesus all the way from Jerusalem far into northwestern Greece. This has all been pioneer work, bringing the Message only into those places where Jesus was not yet known and worshipped. (Romans 15:19, The Message)*

When the apostle Paul penned his letter to the Romans, he was writing, for a change, to a church he had not planted. Despite the fact that he was not the pioneer in this case, he still recognized that he could make a valuable contribution. His involvement was not based simply on whether he had been there first.

The true innovator does not insist on being first at everything. The pioneer spirit is not the same as an independent spirit. Some people want to start everything from scratch, every time. They refuse to invest their

Pioneer Alliances

creativity in something unless they will have the kudos of being first. Great pathfinders, however, don't just start things; they keep them alive – and, sometimes, revive them.

The famed architect and inventor Buckminster Fuller understood this aspect of the pioneer spirit. He suggested that the basic purpose of people on earth is to counteract the tide of entropy that operates all around them. A kettle is quickly brought to the boil when subjected to the energy of a flame or electrical charge. However, it doesn't take long for the water to cool once the flame is extinguished or the plug removed.

The process of entropy affects the world of ideas as much as the natural world. Any good idea, without constant innovation, will naturally tend to wind down. All great strategies and projects need to be exposed to constant outside energy in the form of creativity. That is why the process of adapting ideas is just as important as the process of coming up with new ones. The pioneer spirit applies the flame of fresh innovation to existing ideas and programmes.

Taking it to the Next Level

Manufacturers and advertisers know that any new product or concept, if left to itself, will move through five phases during its lifetime. Innovation is the first phase, where someone has the spark of a fresh idea or approach. For some people, this is the most exciting prospect in life: to be around when a phenomenal new concept is born.

Innovation is certainly an exciting process. Alongside innovation, though, must come adaptation. The original idea or product must be re-tooled to better meet needs – without losing the special core values that made the idea

94   *The Pioneer Spirit*

unique in the first place. When the ideas behind laser technology were first developed, nobody could see an everyday application for them. Innovators had a great idea, but 'adapters' were needed to link the basic technique with everyday needs. Adapters took laser technology and applied it, in CD players and DVD units, for example.

After adaptation, comes maturity. This is where many people have become aware of the product or service. Its name is recognized everywhere and people who were not previously connected to it are now buying into the vision. If you're a pioneer, this is an exhilarating time: when other people, and particularly leaders, are seeing the positive benefits of your idea and bringing their resources in behind it. It's also the time when you start to see how your vision will actually change people's lives.

After maturity, saturation may set in. This is where people take the product for granted and supply begins to outstrip demand. People are a bit too familiar with the idea; it's become a bit ho-hum in the marketplace of life. It's not grabbing the headlines anymore. Once the product gets to this point, it can move into terminal decline. If an idea is allowed to get to that fifth and final stage, its early popularity and momentum become impossible to revive.

Now, none of this is a foregone conclusion. Something that started out with great promise doesn't have to end its days in the shadow of futility. Many ideas or projects avoid saturation and decline altogether. Ideas and products *can* be kept alive, *if* pioneers and adapters work hard to keep fresh innovation flowing. Even when the product is in the maturity phase, enjoying real popularity, there must be a constant flow of creative development and adaptation. *Nothing* must be considered beyond the reach of change – except, that is, for the basic,

Pioneer Alliances

righteous values on which the work is based.

Pioneers are just as important in the maturity phase as they are at the launch of a new concept. Jesus knew the dangers of becoming complacent when we are enjoying success. He said:

> *Woe to you when all men speak well of you, for that is how their fathers treated the false prophets. (Luke 6:26)*

When we enter the maturity phase of a project, we should stay a little wary and watchful. We may start compromising our integrity, or that of the project, to stay popular.

Sometimes, businesses and other groups make the mistake of losing their best pioneers once a programme has taken off. The assumption is that the people who came up with the idea won't be able to see it through to the next level.

Adapters will certainly be needed and, along the way, innovators may well be imported from outside the original design group. Adapters bring new skills to the production process, as well as a wider circle of contacts that can help take the project further. Eventually though, the same minds that devised the idea can help to keep it alive.

Steve Jobs of Apple Computers is a good case in point. One of the pioneers of Apple's success early on, Jobs was replaced as head of the company by those who thought he'd taken is as far as he could. In time, however, it became clear that the company needed his pioneer spirit to revive its flagging place in the market. When the company asked him back, Jobs brought with him a whole swag of interesting, attractive new ideas that have since captured the imagination of many people. He has helped to re-position his company and stave off decline.

96 *The Pioneer Spirit*

Like all pioneers, Jobs also carries a strong passion for the company and the products he helped to create. A pioneer's emotional drive should never be under-estimated. The inventors of any concept carry a special love for it in their hearts, an affection that's not always felt by other people. That love for 'their baby' can drive them to go the extra mile, to make the sacrifices needed to see an idea through. Emotion can lead people to do some astounding things, especially when the odds are stacked against them.

Pioneers need adapters and adapters need pioneers – just as leaders of organisations need gifted admini-strators. Administrators and managers administer, or bring into order, the various aspects of a vision. They give it structure. Without the fire of pioneer spirits, though, there may soon be *nothing left to administer*! Passionate pioneers will fight to avoid disaster long after other people have jumped ship. We throw them overboard at our peril.

There are some parallels here with the life of the church. Different leadership gifts are needed in the early stages of any ministry. Innovation is often the domain of apostolic and prophetic ministries. These two work well together because, as we saw earlier, prophets tend to *see* and identify a preferred future, while apostles *devise a plan* to get people there. Daniel was aware of how God was going to restore Israel, but Nehemiah was the one called to rebuild the walls of Jerusalem. Evangelists are also good innovators, of course, because they carry an old message to a new audience. The art of evangelism, as one preacher put it, is about saying the same thing repeatedly, in new ways.

Apostles, prophets and evangelists are often the ones who break new ground. Pastors and teachers, on the other hand, make great adapters. They are able to take

Pioneer Alliances

what has been planted and water the seed to produce real growth in the lives of everyday people with their very practical concerns. I'm not suggesting that pastors and teachers are not or cannot be creative. Far from it! Without creativity and risk-taking, *no* ministry can thrive or succeed. Yet, if you look back to the beginning of any truly effective ministry, you will normally find the fingerprints of an apostolic, prophetic or evangelistic leader – or, very often, all three.

All five of these ministry gifts are needed in the life of the church across a city. Without them, the body of Christ will never come to spiritual maturity or to its full place of influence in the community. Even in church circles, though, pioneers are sometimes overlooked in the later growth of a movement.

Leaders that follow the pioneers should recognize the special anointing of God that comes with the launching of a work – especially if the pioneer has gone on to start other successful works. A unique spiritual blessing comes to any group of people when they honour those who blazed the trail they now walk. Styles change, priorities change; but a church or ministry that can't appreciate its own roots can never re-dig the wells under its feet.

For their part, of course, pioneers must learn to recognize when it's time to bring in other people. That can be a very difficult process for them: it means they're sharing the care of 'their baby' with someone else. Sometimes, they have to step out of the key leadership role, to play a lesser part. There may also come a time when they need to walk away from direct involvement, so that they can go forth to explore new oceans.

Networks: Common Values and Priorities

Because pioneers build on what others have achieved, they are always on the lookout for strategic relationships. They want to network with other creative thinkers. They know they need to form alliances with like-minded innovators. Often, when an especially close relationship is emerging, pioneer leaders will develop what the Bible calls covenants.

Networks are groups of like-minded people who share a common set of interests or values. Everybody is part of at least one network – that is, the family. Throughout life, we form various kinds of networks. We develop circles of friends, groups of co-workers and families of our own.

Networks are formed around the framework of shared interests and priorities. Networks tend to be non-hierarchical. They tend to grow across an organisation rather than being imposed from above. Many networks occur in an informal way. They come into existence simply because people of like mind discover one another.

The power of informal networking has been impressed upon us again in recent times with the incredible growth of the Internet. The success of the Internet is based on companies, organisations and individuals sharing information and opportunities. Corporations that were once completely closed to each other are now sharing facilities, systems and ideas via the Internet. This provides them with an endgame situation where everyone wins.

At their basic level, networks are informal and natural. They cannot be forced into being, but they can be encouraged. Leaders of organisations can facilitate the forming of networks – across departments, regions, or even industries – so that people experience what the Bible calls 'iron sharpening iron'.[1]

When we are seeking to network 'by design' in this

Pioneer Alliances

way, we must first ensure that we have common priorities on which to build.[2] Over the years, too many leaders and organisations have tried to set up leadership networks without first finding out who shares their fundamental values.

Sadly, attempts at networking between churches and denominations have provided some of the best – or worst – examples of this. A case in point would be some local ministers' fraternal meetings. Originally, I suppose, these were set up with the aim of bringing Christian ministers of different persuasions together for cross-denominational talks. Many of these fraternals originated at times when there were common, city-wide projects to be planned – evangelistic campaigns, for example.

Over time, however, many of them have lost their edge, because they haven't kept in focus a set of values or practical priorities. At many of their meetings, promoting the gospel and making disciples for Christ have taken a back seat to discussions about politics, economics and even sport! In such cases, networks that might have played a positive role in lifting the churches' community influence have become nothing more than glorified coffee mornings – something that every good leader with a busy schedule is desperate to avoid.

If there are no common priorities between people, nothing is accomplished. If the only objective leaders share is that they should not offend one another, the network won't last long enough to be of any benefit. Without honesty and authenticity, people can never experience the real benefits of networking.

While networking will happen automatically throughout our lives – in the background, as it were – there are seasons when we'll deliberately invest more time in it. Sometimes, we know that we need to stretch our circle of peers – to increase our knowledge base and

100 *The Pioneer Spirit*

re-fire our enthusiasm through contact with new people. So, we go looking for networks to join or we facilitate some new ones of our own. We invite different people to our conferences; we send our materials to a larger contact group, and so on. This also has the effect of widening our level of influence, as more people are exposed to our gifts and expertise.

Well-structured networks can provide opportunities for people to develop friendships and to share resources. They bring more people into a decision-making process. More importantly, they provide a launching pad for strategic alliances and even, over time, covenant relationships.

In business and church life, networks that are effective usually take on a more organized and formal expression over time. They don't, however, need to become constitutional bodies or institutions. Too much structure is the death knell for a network. The bottom line is this: you can facilitate a network, but you really can't create it. Networking is about people of common interest finding each other.

Alliances: Common Vision and Strategy

Alliances are more than friendships or acquaintances, or even networks. They are much more strategic and deliberate.

Alliances are partnerships that are formed for a clearly defined purpose. At the centre of every alliance there is a core belief and value system, and a clear goal. Sometimes, alliances are formed between people groups that have nothing else in common aside from that central goal. Often, an alliance will only last as long as it takes to get a certain job done.

During the Second World War, Winston Churchill

Pioneer Alliances

made an alliance with Joseph Stalin. Churchill had very little in common with Stalin. Their values were vastly different, as history shows. Yet, for the sake of the overall goal – the defeat of Hitler – Churchill was willing to put aside personal feelings. Other alliances, such as that with Franklin Roosevelt, were much more comfortable for Churchill, but this one, too, was necessary to the cause.

Christian pioneer leaders will sometimes form alliances with people and organisations outside of the church. There are many important changes to be made in society: changes that cannot be made by one church acting alone. Sometimes, church leaders will work with other community groups to achieve the specific task at hand. For example, many churches work hand in hand with government-funded, secular rehabilitation groups in order to alleviate drug abuse in their communities. In some countries, churches work with government agencies to set up schools.

For a pioneer leader, it can sometimes appear easier to go it alone rather than working with others. However, we often make a much bigger impact, and leave a more lasting legacy, when we work within alliances.

Some years back, Pastor Ray McCauley of South Africa told me how he and other key pastors had started building alliances so that they could begin to place a born-again Christian chaplain in every police station throughout their nation. This was a bold, pioneer strategy. To begin with, the pastors built alliances within the Christian community, forming links across denominational lines. Once that was achieved, they began to work with secular authorities in different places.

At every step along the way, the pioneers of the idea were willing to share ownership of the idea with others. They allowed outside input without compromising the central goals, which were to change the lives of young

The Pioneer Spirit

offenders and to bring down the rising crime rate. None of the churches or organisations involved could possibly have achieved the goal working on their own. They needed each other – and the wider community needed them to work together.

Abraham and Isaac made alliances, or treaties, with pagan kings. These kings did not share their faith in God, but the treaties were made for the common good. The alliances prevented the breakout of hostilities between Abraham's people and those of surrounding nations. Under the protection of those treaties, Abraham and Isaac were free to get on with their covenant business under God.

Sadly, in the Christian world, we have not always been comfortable developing alliances with other Christians – much less with secular powers. However, we will need to work together if we are to reverse the tide of post-modern thinking and place Christian truth back on the social agenda. New churches will need to learn to work together with older churches. Established churches will need to make room for younger churches in their district. Both have unique strengths to offer the other. Both have needs the other can meet.

New churches are strong in vision and can-do mentality. Their leaders and people have a passion for change and for contemporary forms of expression. Because they are less entrenched in tradition, their people tend to be more easily motivated and mobilized for new projects. Having fewer layers of leadership and less constitutional process to work through also means that decision-making tends to be quicker for new churches than for their more established counterparts.

Older churches, on the other hand, possess more established networks with other church groups. They will also tend to be better known in the community as a whole, especially if they have an evangelical history.

Pioneer Alliances

They often have better financial reserves and deeper pockets, too. And taking longer to reach decisions can sometimes mean that older churches are less easily distracted once a process of change gets started.

It doesn't take a rocket scientist to figure out that a new and an old church can both benefit by forming a strategic alliance. Of course, each will learn to accommodate the different decision-making processes of the other.

This is one of the perennial challenges facing a pioneer leader: enlisting the support of established systems, without becoming entangled in bureaucratic red tape and time wasting. By nature, pioneers are divergent thinkers. They want to challenge the established view, to explore new ways of doing things, to attempt the new and adventurous. Large or long-standing organisations, on the other hand, tend to be more convergent in their approach to questions and problems. They want to get to an answer as quickly as possible, within a more narrowly defined set of parameters. They usually prefer to use a tried and proven system than to invent a new solution.

As the leader of a mobile international mission, I confess to finding many older, denominational organisations challenging to work with. Our decision-making happens quickly and with the involvement of relatively few people. Their systems, however, require that leaders work through more layers of accountability before a choice can be made or a policy changed. In our own case, we've been able, by God's grace, to build alliances with some of Europe's most influential local churches, including some relatively old ones. This has required of us a willingness to make space, to leave time for a slower pace of change.

I'm sure that some of our alliance partners have found working with us a challenge, too. We want to move forward quickly on everything. Yet, when each of us has made room for the other, the synergy has been wonder-

104   *The Pioneer Spirit*

ful. We have seen results that would never have come without these alliances.

Old and new organisations can benefit from alliances. Churches and missions *can* function well side-by-side; church plants *can* co-exist with entrenched congregations. The Kingdom of God is not an either/or proposition. If they can agree on what the preferred future of their city or region looks like – at least in a few areas – new and old, mobile and static organisations can work together to produce some exciting results. Together, they can meet strength-to-weakness and bring about real change.

Covenants: Shared Destiny

Every great endeavour for God is a product of teamwork. The Great Commission is a collective mandate. Jesus' command to 'Go', was given to a group of disciples, not to an individual. Great enterprises, however, have a way of stretching relationships to the limit. The greater the venture, the bigger the risks, the more important are the relationships. That's why, alongside alliances and networks, pioneer leaders need covenant relationships.

A true covenant partner will be around in the bad times as well as the good. In his paraphrase of the New Testament, *The Message*, Eugene Peterson has defined a covenant partner as a 'deep-spirited friend'.[3]

A while ago, there was a great commercial showing on British TV. A young man and woman were seated in a restaurant. The waiter had just taken their order and left their table. You could see that the woman was mustering up her courage to say something. She obviously had a difficult announcement to make.

'John,' she blurted, 'there's . . . there's something I've been meaning to tell you . . . Um . . . I've found someone

Pioneer Alliances 105

else. I'm sorry, but this is the end of the road for us.'

She sank back in her chair, exhausted. Her friend looked at her then silently bowed his head. His shoulders slumped. In the second or two of silence that followed, you could really feel his pain. Then, suddenly, he looked up as a huge grin broke out across his face.

'Yes . . . well . . .' he said, 'I've just won the Lottery!'

Sometimes, we give up on friendships far too quickly! We don't stay around long enough to enjoy the full benefits. That's especially true of the highest form of friendship – a covenant relationship.

Covenant is the most potent form of relationship mentioned in the Bible. The rites of all ancient cultures featured some kind of covenant ceremony. It seems that human beings have always understood the power of this special type of confederacy. In many tribal groups, two parties to a contract would exchange clothing and weapons, before making a solemn blood agreement. The blood signified that the covenant could not be broken except by death.

All of life's most meaningful relationships are represented in the Bible as covenants. Take marriage, for example. Scripture considers marriage to be much more than a legal formality or a piece of paper. Marriage is the product of a binding promise made between two people, before God; it is the joining of a man and a woman so that they live and act as one well-rounded unit, as one whole;[4] it is built upon a pledge of commitment, loyalty and fidelity. Marriage is founded upon a sacred covenant.

Some of the deepest friendships in the Bible were also covenant relationships. Abraham shared a covenant with Lot. David's friendship with Jonathan – one of the most profound in the Bible – was founded on a covenant.

What's more, according to the Bible, the highest form of friendship a man or woman can have with God is a

106 *The Pioneer Spirit*

covenant. Abraham inherited great wealth and influence because God made a covenant with him.[5] The same covenant favour made Isaac a prosperous man. Because of God's covenant with Jacob, his name was changed and with it his character. He turned from being a fugitive into a prince.[6] God made covenant promises to David and from his heirs came the family line of the Messiah. The whole nation of Israel was called into covenant with God. They were set apart to make God's name great in the earth, as he blessed and protected them.[7]

There are many great covenants mentioned in the Bible. By far the most significant, though, is the one that Jesus called the 'New Covenant'. Jesus did not simply launch a new organisation or a new law for living. He established a new covenant, a new agreement of peace and blessing between God and men. He made peace between heaven and earth, fulfilling the terms of the covenant with his life's blood.[8] That's how valuable covenants are to God – he gave his dearest and best for a covenant.

Because of Christ, we can not only be God's friends, we can also be his covenant partners. Kenneth Copeland has defined covenant as 'a promise to give until it is too good to be true.' That's an apt description of what we have through Christ. For me, Paul sums it up in a nutshell, in Ephesians 2:6–7:

Now God has us where he wants us, with all the time in this world and the next to shower grace and kindness on us in Christ Jesus. (The Message)

It's incredible to think that you and I can enjoy the kind of covenant with God that others like Abraham, blessed though they were, could only dream about! Through Christ, we have a better covenant than the covenant of Abraham, because it is built on better promises.[9]

Pioneer Alliances

One important feature of all Bible covenants was that each party tied his or her destiny to that of the other. In other words, if their covenant partner was a success, they could expect to share in the rewards. On the other hand, if their partner went through times of need, they'd be expected to share what was theirs. A party to a covenant couldn't lose: they'd either share the fruits of another's success or they'd experience the joy of helping a friend. That's a good way to live.

The amazing thing is this: by making a covenant with you and me, God has tied our destinies with his! Your future, my future, is bound up with his. If he is successful, you and I will be successful. That's not a bad deal, given that God cannot fail!

Sadly, though, many Christians seem unable to appreciate the amazing potency of their covenant with God. Perhaps that's because we live in an age where covenants get such bad press.

These days, covenants of all kinds have been devalued. People break covenants all the time, usually because one party or the other claims to have outgrown the relationship. Marriages often fall apart, for example, because one partner says, 'I've grown since we were married. I've moved on. I don't need you any more.' When I make a covenant, however, I am making a commitment of total loyalty. I am saying: 'I tie my destiny to yours in a bond of undying loyalty.'

A covenant is a relationship built around absolute fidelity. In Bible times, covenants were always the result of great discussions and deliberations. They were never entered into lightly. Covenant represented the total giving of oneself to another, for life.

In Bible terms, a true covenant partner puts in a good word for you when you're not around to defend yourself;[10] a true covenant partner warns you of trouble

108 *The Pioneer Spirit*

ahead, even at great personal cost;[11] a true covenant partner is willing to be ostracized and even persecuted for his or her association with you;[12] a true covenant partner will remember the friendship even as years go by and memories dim.[13]

In making a covenant, one person was effectively saying to the other: 'Whenever you are weak, I will be your strength. If you are poor, I will provide for you. If you are in a fight, you'll find me standing by your side. When you are wrong, I will rebuke you – in love, and for your own sake. When you are criticized and misunderstood, I will stand up for you. If people say you're finished and they come to bury you, I'll take the flowers from the grave and raise you up again.'

We shouldn't keep covenants only for as long as we feel they're equal. Abraham had much more to lose than Lot when they entered into a covenant. Jonathan had more to lose than David when they made their famous covenant. Jesus certainly had more to lose than I did when he went to the cross for me.

We keep covenants even when they're not equal, because that is what God has done for us. He is a covenant-honouring God and he blesses those who respect covenants. Empty promises are the way of the world, but *keeping* covenant is the way of heaven.

Unlike alliances, covenants don't stay in place only for as long as both parties are in total agreement. That's because they're not established solely on common values or shared strategies. They're rooted in a common destiny.

Another feature of Bible covenants was that they were based not just on what people had in common, but on the mix of strengths and weaknesses between them. A covenant enabled one party to cover for the weaknesses or deficiencies of the other. Each of us needs people in our lives who will do the same.

Pioneer Alliances

A very special kind of favour comes upon my life when I learn to keep covenant just as God does. Of course, what the other party does with their covenant promise is their responsibility but I must do everything within my power to live up to mine. The world needs to see a radical return to covenant Christianity, where people of faith keep their sacred promises and rediscover the beauty of the covenant.

Great pioneers cannot function alone. They don't try to. Innovators look for networks with people of similar values, where they can exchange resources and discover new approaches. They seek out strategic alliances with people and groups of like mind and heart with whom they can work, plan and achieve specific goals.

Pioneers also invest time and effort in building covenant relationships: friendships that will stand the test of time and hold up in the heat of battle. Without networks, alliances and covenants, pioneering can be a dangerous and demoralising enterprise. With them, pathfinders can keep their fire alive and their vision intact.

1. Proverbs 27:17
2. Amos 3:3
3. Philippians 2:2, *The Message*
4. Genesis 2:24
5. Genesis 24:35
6. Genesis 32:28
7. Leviticus 26:12
8. Matthew 26:26
9. Hebrews 8:6
10. 1 Samuel 19:4
11. See 1 Samuel 20
12. 1 Samuel 20:32–33
13. 2 Samuel 9:6–11

7

Pioneering: What a Ride!

There's nothing more exciting or fulfilling in this life than being present when God starts something new! I know that from experience.

Throughout the 1980s and early 1990s, I was privileged to lead a movement in our nation known as Youth Alive Australia. What started with just three hundred young people grew in just ten or so years to represent well over fifty thousand across the nation. It touched young people's lives in schools, universities and churches, and brought thousands to Christ in large outreach events.

Personally, I don't spend too much time looking over my shoulder, except to thank God for his faithfulness. There are too many good things happening in the 'now' to be preoccupied with the 'back then'! But in recent days, many people in Australia, in Europe and elsewhere have been asking me about the early days of the Youth Alive Australia phenomenon.

I felt that somewhere in this book the Lord wanted me to answer some of those questions, to illustrate how pioneers can work with God to create something wonderful. Hopefully, in the process, I can inspire others to take risks for Jesus.

Pioneering: What a Ride! 111

So, to encourage all the pioneers out there, here's just a small slice from the incredible story that is Youth Alive Australia. It's not the whole story – that would fill a book of its own. This is just an excerpt from the very earliest days.

There are many important names that won't feature in this tiny snippet. The story is still being written, as a new generation of leaders takes the ministry to new heights. But this is a part of it . . .

Imagine for a moment that you were a painter or a sculptor and someone offered you the chance to watch Michelangelo at work. Would you take it? Of course you would! You'd grab the opportunity with both hands – and probably both feet, as well.

Now, how would it be if Michelangelo, the master, invited you to actually assist him – to help him create a masterpiece? What if you could work as his apprentice, under his personal supervision?

God has offered you and me an opportunity that makes that one appear lame by comparison! He is the master pioneer; the supreme innovator; the one who is ultimately behind *every* great idea. We've been specially selected not just to watch him work, but to come alongside as his apprentices. We can have some of his genius rub off on us. What better way could there be to learn the art of innovation?

Early in our ministry lives, my wife Davina and I watched from the box seats as God birthed a phenomenal youth movement called Youth Alive Australia. Much of it started back in 1981, at an Easter youth camp in the coastal town of Portsea, Victoria.

I'll never forget that camp. Three hundred young people had come together from churches across our state. Easter camps had been happening for a long time in our

112 *The Pioneer Spirit*

part of the country. For years, our denomination had run a youth programme, state-by-state. When I came into youth leadership, though, our state ministry had changed very little since my father was a teenager! It was colourless, powerless and certainly didn't do a lot to reach my generation. Frankly, I felt embarrassed to bring people to the few events we had in a year.

In the months leading up to Easter of 1981, things began to change. The events of that Easter camp were, in many ways, the culmination of a process; a momentum that had been building in some youth groups for months. Members of the youth group I was leading, which was growing rapidly at the time, had been praying and fasting for months, seeking God's face for breakthroughs. We'd also been out doing street evangelism with the kind of fervour churches hadn't seen for years.

We weren't the only ones. The same hunger for prayer and evangelism was being felt right across our state. Leaders wanted to do more than run predictable meetings for comfortable Christians. We wanted to change our world. We actually believed what the apostle Paul said:

[God] is able to do immeasurably more than all we ask or imagine, according to his power that is at work within us. (Ephesians 3:20)

Looking back, I have to tell you that our Easter camp in 1981 was primitive by today's standards. The music wasn't *Top of the Pops* material – though it *was* loud – and there wasn't a lot of sophistication about the skills of our leadership team. We were learning as we went along. But we started taking some risks; changing things that many people would have been happier to have stay the same. That opened the door a crack – just enough for the Holy Spirit to get his foot inside!

Pioneering: What a Ride! 113

That weekend turned out to be significant for several reasons. For one thing, it was the first time any youth groups in our nation had come together under the name Youth Alive – though it was, at that stage, only within our state. This in itself caused a stir: some people wanted to keep the old name, one that had no meaning to our generation.

Far more significant, though, was the incredible spiritual atmosphere that seemed to blanket the camp. No, I'm not going to tell you that everyone saw visions of heaven, heard the Hallelujah Chorus in their sleep and kept falling down in the parking lot! Every meeting, though, was alive with a sense of anticipation – and it had nothing to do with hype. We were hungry for God and we could sense that something special was starting to build.

All kinds of signs followed the preaching that weekend. People were healed and delivered from demonic powers. Others were laid out by power of the Holy Spirit. Some of them looked like they had been picked up by an invisible hand and thrown backwards. A few people reported having visions of angels and many people made a commitment to Christ for the first time. There was a great release of prophetic gifts, too. Several times over those few days, we were told that God had ignited a small spark that would soon flare into flames across the nation.

Some of my strongest memories of that camp, though, feature the meal times. Often, more than half of the places at the tables remained empty. (No, the food was *not* that bad!) When we went in search of the campers, we found many of them gathered on the football ground or in the camp hospital, crying out to God in loud, aggressive prayer. When the weekend ended, we were all exhausted, but few people came away without a sense that something big was building!

114 *The Pioneer Spirit*

Around that time, youth groups like our own had started holding outreach events that combined performance, worship and in-your-face preaching. We moved out of churches and hired secular halls, because we wanted to get the gospel to kids on their turf.

After the '81 Easter camp, youth leaders came together to do the same thing across the entire city, and the state. Together, we started taking some major risks. We brought in new music styles and hired the best equipment we could afford. We preached with passion and made a clear call for kids to lay down their lives for Christ. We started promoting the events in schools. We also took some real financial risks.

Faith always requires that we stretch the budget to the limit. God wants us to offer him projects that require his supernatural supply. Without that faith element, there's no room for making God famous!

Of course, other Christian organisations in our city were running events at the same time. For the most part, though, these offered little more than alternative Christian entertainment. There's nothing wrong with entertainment – far from it. If God is in a thing, it *will* be entertaining. However, young people in our churches were desperate for something more than that. They wanted an in-your-face presentation of Jesus' message, in an excellent package. They wanted something that didn't compromise the gospel, but was good enough for them to bring friends to. They wanted a place where they could worship God with passion and *feel* his presence. They were hungry for a call to live heroically, to change their world.

Our events started to grow and we started to fill venues. At first, we had a few hundred in each event, then over a thousand, and then two thousand. Scores of young people were coming to Christ for the first time.

Pioneering: What a Ride!

Youth groups began bussing kids in from across the state. Some would drive for four hours or more just for a two-hour event.

At the same time, there was opposition to what we were doing. Sometimes, we'd get letters from pastors who questioned the kind of music we were playing, or the style of our preaching, or the way we used lighting and sound equipment. I remember the letters we received about using 'coloured lights' and dry-ice machines on stage! (What's the world coming to? Flashing lights and smoke in church?! Actually, God loves to use both – check out the Old Testament.)

It's hard to believe now: when Youth Alive uses the biggest, the best and the most expensive technology and equipment and even local churches have gone high-tech.

Some youth leaders opposed us, too. Many of their young people would turn up at the events anyway, because they were hungry for God. Gradually, though, church leaders became excited and supportive as Youth Alive grew beyond anyone's expectations. We had already started to attract attention from key Christian leaders across the nation.

In 1985, we invited one of Australia's most respected Christian leaders to preach for us. Though he was no longer a young man, Pastor Frank Houston had more passion and raw energy than many sixteen-year-olds. That night, we'd taken another step of faith. We had booked a venue we thought we'd struggle to fill. In the end, though, the building was so full that we had people sitting on the fire escapes and in the stairwells. Frank preached his heart out and many people came forward to accept Jesus.

A couple of days later, Frank returned to his church in Sydney. He couldn't stop talking about what he'd seen. He challenged his ministry team: 'If these Melbourne

116   *The Pioneer Spirit*

guys can do this, *we* certainly can!' A creative evangelist working with Frank's team went from that meeting to launch youth outreach events in Sydney. He gave them the name Youth Alive, but he soon handed the leadership to a guy who was destined to take the Sydney events to great heights – Pat Mesiti.

Under Pat's leadership, the Sydney events later became, for a time, the benchmark in the nation. They gave new meaning to the words 'On a Mission from God'. Pat especially lifted the vision for evangelism in high schools across Australia.

At the same time, Youth Alive ministries were forming in Brisbane and Adelaide, under the pioneer leadership of Wayne Alcorn and Danny Guglielmucci respectively. One of the great things about Youth Alive Australia has been the way each city has spurred on the others. When one leader would report a great crowd and big results, all the others would feel motivated to go out and do better! There's nothing wrong with a little competition, as long as we keep it in check so that it serves the right purpose – making *God* famous.

In the late 1970s, church planting and evangelism had become the central passion of Australian church leaders, especially in the Pentecostal and Charismatic wings of the church. God was now raising up a brand of young people who could *do* church planting and evangelism. It was an exciting time to be around.

Every truly effective pioneer venture builds on the work of others who've gone before. Without the visionary approach of some of the senior leaders in our denomination, we could not have grown – at least beyond a certain point. I thank God that older men were willing to release us, without too many hindrances, to reach our generation.

In 1986, I invited Pat, Wayne and Danny, along with

Pioneering: What a Ride! 117

some other key leaders, to join me for a summit in Melbourne. Our goal was simple: to see a national alliance of youth leaders and young people who were passionate about reaching a generation for Christ. We took a radical idea to that two-day meeting: the formation of a national movement under the banner of Youth Alive. We didn't ask anyone's permission or wait for anyone's approval – though I did make sure the leaders of our denomination were well informed. We knew that God was in this – that it was the right idea at the right time.

After two days of strategic planning, prayer and prophecy – and a lot of laughter – Youth Alive Australia was born. I was asked to be the national director and the leadership team was made up of the directors of Youth Alive in each state. We wanted this movement to be accessible to Christians of all persuasions. We wanted to raise up leaders who could serve a new generation. We were desperate to see God's Spirit at work among young people, on an unprecedented scale. The rest, as they say, is history . . .

A Pioneer Alliance

Every person on the first Youth Alive Australia national team was immensely gifted. Each one had a highly developed sense of purpose, as well as a strong stubborn streak. As you can imagine, there were times when we disagreed on principle and others when, well, our egos clashed! In the years that followed, we didn't always see eye-to-eye, but we did maintain a respect and affection for each other. We determined not just to be co-workers – we were friends. We laughed together, we dreamed together, we competed with each other, and we some-times cried together.

118 *The Pioneer Spirit*

None of us knew the others well before we joined hands in this strategy. Initially, common values and a shared vision brought us together. However, other things were needed to keep us together: namely, a strong sense of friendship, a passion for a generation and the knowledge that we *needed* each other if we were to reach our individual potential. That commitment, that sense of teamwork, seemed to carry down through every level of Youth Alive.

As a leadership team, we started with a network based on common values. That progressed quickly to an alliance built upon common vision and co-dependency. In the end, though, the whole process brought some of us into covenant relationships. I know that we have let each other down at times, but when you make the decision to stay in good relationship no matter what, it can carry you through anything.

Reconciliation is the heart of Jesus Christ. Christians should do everything they can to preserve relationships, no matter what the pain along the way. Joseph kept a clean spirit, even when he was faced with years in prison for a crime he didn't commit. That attitude brought the favour of God into his life.

It's amazing what God can do in a short time, if innovators are willing to form alliances. All kinds of adventurous plans were hatched during the two-day summit meeting in Melbourne. Out of it came a Youth Alive national magazine, a Youth Alive leadership conference and early plans for Youth Alive training schools, among other things.

After this, the national team met twice each year. Each of the ideas initiated at the first meeting was developed further over the next few years, as other creative leaders were brought into the decision-making arena. Some of these strategies have since 'gone the way of all flesh'.

Pioneering: What a Ride! 119

Others have been morphed into new forms. Yet, the pioneer fire that marked that first national team continues to burn in the hearts of Youth Alive leaders today.

After the formation of Youth Alive as a national body, youth events took off across Australia. In the state capitals, events were soon drawing between four and ten thousand young people. Scores and then hundreds of young people were coming to Christ in each event.

My friends and I, all of us in our mid-twenties, would stand on huge stages, in major concert and sporting venues, wondering how we'd got there. Pioneer passion is not enough on its own – we need the favour of God to carry the vision through. We'd watch with tears in our eyes as young people rushed to get to the front for prayer. On any given night, you'd see people of all persuasions with their hands raised to the sky, praising God with everything they had in them. Skinheads, goths, punks, surfers, metalheads, skaters and everyone in between – all would stand united around one incredible person – Jesus.

All the while, huge buildings were being filled in Australia's major cities. Even theme parks fell victim to Youth Alive! Youth Alive produced the first live recordings of Australian worship. Albums like *Totally Radical* and *Shake This City* predated the now famous *Hillsong* recordings. Some of the musicians, who gained acclaim for the latter, worked with Youth Alive in the early days.

Youth Alive also grew quickly outside the major capitals. In regional cities, youth events of two thousand people and more were soon becoming commonplace. Soon, the vision spread into New Zealand. We were able to stand with pioneer leaders in that great country, to lift the passion for youth ministry there.

Because of the growth, we saw attitudes to youth

120   *The Pioneer Spirit*

leadership change. Being a youth pastor was once seen as a second-class career; now it was a first-class calling. Youth Alive launched a whole range of leadership training schools, conferences and seminars that promoted contemporary leadership – long before that subject became popular in church circles.

Families were impacted by Youth Alive and churches were changed. Pastors suddenly found that they had bands of motivated world-beaters sitting in their Sunday meetings. Youth Alive also changed the style of presentation in many churches, as young people released their music, preaching and leadership gifts. Churches were able to benefit from music gifts, instead of losing them to clubs and pubs!

Youth Alive events also deeply affected many of the people who were employed to work on them. I especially remember the story of one particular security guard. He approached the local leaders after one of our events.

'Would you pray for me?' he said, tears streaming down his face. 'Something's happened to me tonight. I need Jesus in my life.'

When they'd prayed, they talked to him for a while and then asked, 'What was it about tonight that really touched you? Was it the music, the preaching, or what?'

'No,' he replied. 'That was all great . . . but . . . no, that wasn't the thing that really got me.'

'What was it then?' they pressed.

'It was the kids,' he replied, crying again. 'You see, I've done security at all the big shows in this town. I've seen all the big acts . . . But I've *never* known young people to respond to *anything* like they did tonight! When they started coming to the front, in the hundreds, I couldn't stop crying . . . They came from the balconies, from the back of the auditorium, from everywhere! Something just happened inside me. I knew I needed Jesus, too.'

Pioneering: What a Ride! 121

Every leader of every event could tell you similar stories that would fill whole books.

After every event, leaders across the nation reported that young people had been added to their churches. We knew, as many prominent overseas visitors told us, that what we were witnessing was more than the growth of a movement. This was a *phenomenon*, a 'God thing'!

Structure Without Control

As Youth Alive continued to grow, we tried not to package it too much. Pioneer leaders should try to define what they're doing right – that way they can share the key principles with others. They should also bring a structure to what they're doing. Without it, growth cannot be sustained. I once asked a well-known Australian evangelist what was the major difference between Youth Alive and the Australian Jesus movement of the late sixties. He answered with one word: 'Structure . . . We had none!'

As pioneer leaders we can, however, add too much structure if we're not careful. When that happens, the spark of creativity is stifled by the cold water of control. We start tying our own self-esteem too closely to the success of the work. When that happens, we become more concerned about our image than we are about God's name. We stop taking risks, for fear of losing face. We also lose our enthusiasm for bringing new leaders into the project because we're afraid of losing our authority.

If leaders try to become superstars on the back of something that *God* has done, it is dishonouring to him. After a while, he reluctantly takes away his hand of favour, or he raises up someone else to finish the job. It *is* a healthy thing to brag about what God is doing – just as long as we're boasting about *him*!

122 *The Pioneer Spirit*

In its structure, Youth Alive Australia has always operated with a close, genetic link to local churches. To this day, most of the key Youth Alive leaders are youth pastors in churches, or youth evangelists or apostles linked to churches. Youth Alive Australia works like a very large network, within which leaders have developed alliances and covenant relationships.

Since the early trailblazing days of Youth Alive Australia, a new generation of leaders has stepped in to drive the vision forward and to adapt it to current needs. Yet, the basic values remain the same, and the pioneer passion lives on.

Today, our national tennis centre is filled to capacity every time Youth Alive books it for a night. It seats fifteen thousand people. The Youth Alive Australia model for outreach and training is utilized in countries around the world and it has given rise to other major initiatives, including the incredible *Planet Shakers* events.

When I look back at what God did in the formative years of Youth Alive in my homeland, I feel a great sense of gratitude and satisfaction. I was honoured to be involved. However, I also feel very challenged. I want to live to be a part of even bigger things. Thank God, that's already happening – and the best is yet to come!

I'm sure that you have the same desire – to gather momentum so that one success in God leads you to believe for an even bigger one. That's the thing about pioneers: they don't spend too much time looking over their shoulders. What did the apostle Paul say?

Forgetting what is behind and straining toward what is ahead, I press on toward the goal to win the prize for which God has called me . . . (Philippians 3:13–14)

In the words of that immortal philosopher, Anonymous, 'We ain't seen nothin' yet!'

He taught them many things by parables . . .

St Mark

I will open my mouth in parables, I will utter
hidden things, things from of old.

Asaph, Master Musician

The medium is the message.

Marshall McLuhan

Nothing is taught
Until something is learned.

Anonymous

From TV and radio, to movies and the ubiquitous Internet, there can be no denying the power of the electronic media in our day-to-day lives.

If we as Christians are to have an impact, to make God famous in this post-modern world, we will need to become pioneers again. We will need to plant seeds of the good news in all the major spheres of influence in our world, just as the apostle Paul did in his.

Each book in this series features a special section. In it, we will look at one sphere in which I believe Christians and churches *can* exercise influence. In book one of the series, the subject was Christians and the arts. Here, it is another topic close to my heart – Christian influence in the media.

I know, from my many travels around the world, that a growing number of Christians feel a call to be involved, at some level, with the electronic media. Perhaps you are one of them. You may be gifted in TV production, writing, radio production, movie direction, animation, videography, web design, music composition, advertising, or a host of other related skills. The next chapters are definitely for you!

On the other hand, you might be thinking, 'That's not for me. I'm no TV star.' Well, you probably use the Internet and you almost certainly watch TV and movies or listen to the radio. So, the electronic media are an important part of your life. In any case, this section is as much about communication as it is about media. I hope you'll find something here that will help lift your communication skills to a higher level, so that you can become a pioneer for truth in this desperately uncertain age.

Mal Fletcher

8

Jesus On the Airwaves

It's July 1969. Here in one of the grade six classrooms at my school, it's hard to believe that man will shortly set foot on the moon.

A TV set sits on a table at the front of the classroom and all eyes are glued on the grainy, black and white picture. There's an almost tangible excitement in the air as we shuffle about in our seats in eager anticipation.

Suddenly, there it is on-screen: the lunar module, 'The Eagle', with its stepladder lowered to the lunar surface. We can just make out Neil Armstrong, at first only in silhouette against the brightly-lit horizon. Now the picture takes on more detail as the camera lens adjusts to the light.

Armstrong is moving carefully down the ladder, unable to look down in his helmet and bulky suit. Then, a pause . . . and his boot touches down on lunar dust.

'That's one small step for man, one giant leap for mankind,' he declares. Very poetic.

Those words and pictures will be forever etched on the minds of my classmates and I. Just as they will on the minds of millions of other eager viewers who have watched this miracle taking place, 'live', with the help of another wonder of the age – television.

128 *The Pioneer Spirit*

Baby boomers the world over clearly remember the first time they saw TV pictures of such world-shaking events as the assassination of President Kennedy, or the moon landing of Apollo 11.

GenXers may look back on the first Internet broadcast of a baby's birth, or the opening of their first web pages or email accounts. A century ago, the world went through an industrial revolution. Today, we are in the middle of an information revolution and the media has unprecedented influence in shaping our thinking and values.

Of course, the word 'media' simply refers to means or agencies for communication. However, we've come to use the word in a much more specific sense. We use it as if we were talking about a single entity or something that has a life of its own.

When the Beatles performed on the Ed Sullivan show in the early sixties, seventy million people tuned in to watch. It was one of the largest TV audiences up to that time. Back then, media communication was still much more print- and text-based and TV was something that existed at the periphery of people's lives.

These days, the electronic media – TV, radio, film and the powerful Internet – influence just about every area of our lives: business, finance, entertainment, news and much more. We pay our bills online, we read the newspaper on our mobile phones, and we talk to each other in electronic 'chat rooms' – without even opening our mouths!

From Small Things Big Things Grow ...

Samuel Morse first tried to transmit electromagnetic messages over wires way back in 1844, yet radio broadcasting didn't kick off until around 1920. Radio

Jesus On the Airwaves

129

may have had a slow start, but from that time on, the sky was the limit.

The development of transistors made radio what it is today: a communication medium still unequalled in its global reach. It is more economical than other electronic media. In recent years, we've even seen the invention of manually powered (wind up) radios for people who live in remote areas and have no access to electricity. It may also be more personal than TV or movies.

While radio was taking off, testing had begun on another new medium – television. The first TV stations took to the air in the 1930s and, though World War II slowed its development for a while, TV exploded once the war ended. By 1948, there were thirty-six TV stations on air in the US alone, with more than a million receivers. Networks sprang up in the late 1940s and TV went 'full colour' in 1966.

From the beginning, TV production in the US was commercially based, in line with American capitalist culture. In Europe, the flagship TV institutions were state-funded. In the past three decades, the introduction of cable and satellite transmission has meant that programmes produced in one country can be beamed across the globe in an instant. Live news coverage has made the world seem a smaller place, and interactive TV-phone-email programmes are allowing viewers to question and talk back to the newsmakers.

Alongside radio and TV, film has also played an important role in the development of western culture. Thomas Edison produced the first motion pictures in 1896 when he recorded the inauguration of President William McKinley. Edison's invention has since become a multi-billion dollar industry. Its tentacles are spread from Hollywood to Bombay, from Cannes to Melbourne.

The impact of film has a lot to do with its ability to draw us into a story. It is able to enlist two of our most

130 *The Pioneer Spirit*

potent senses at once, sight and sound, to evoke emotions. Communications and media expert Viggo Sorgaard writes: 'Few media are more persuasive than film. As the viewer relaxes in a darkened theatre or room, he or she becomes a participant in the field of action on the screen and experiences the full range of emotions as the story unfolds. Limited effort is demanded of the viewer.'[1]

Ads and Apples

A recent study found that 87 per cent of boys say they'd rather watch TV and videos in their spare time than play sport. A good proportion of that can be attributed to the power of media advertising.

Global advertising giants have grown hand-in-hand with the big TV and film conglomerates. They've facilitated the spread of western products like Coca-Cola, Pepsi and McDonalds into China. Advertising may at times be a proverbial pain-in-the-neck, but, as Muggeridge noted, it is 'the price we pay for freedom of the press . . . It's the freedom [we] want, not the advertising, which is only a means (and a very imperfect, sometimes distasteful, means) to an end.'[2]

Perhaps the greatest wonder of our media age is the computer. When Alan Turing harnessed the power of electronics to build the first computers, he couldn't possibly have foreseen the explosion in computer technology we're witnessing today. It's impossible to estimate the number of people who surf the net or fire email messages around the world, across strings of optical fibre. Internet software mega-companies have sprung up overnight, making instant millionaires of computer programmers. One of the world's richest men, Bill Gates, is probably the ultimate computer nerd-turned-mogul.

Jesus On the Airwaves

Today, computers control so many of our daily services and tools: from phone calls and credit accounts, to supermarket payments and factory equipment. When the first cumbersome business computers appeared in the 1950s, they often filled whole rooms. Nowadays, they fit snugly into briefcases and handbags. Hand-held machines can contain up to one hundred thousand pages of text – the equivalent of three hundred books. Fashion companies are even launching computer-enhanced clothes, or 'wearable computers'.

The key to every computer's processing power is the microchip. It was invented in 1958. Before that time, there were only a few computers in existence and they ran on transistors, valves and switches. Microchips are tiny technological wonders. Just a quarter of an inch square, each one is imprinted with millions of microscopic switches and connecting wires.

Next to the microchip, probably the greatest recent advances in computer technology have been made in the area of fibre-optics. Networks of computers are connected by fibre-optic cables the width of a human hair. Each fibre can potentially carry billions of characters of information per second, across vast distances.

Computer technology is developing at such a pace that the question 'When will my computer be out of date?' is usually answered with, 'When you take it out of the store!' Over the next few years, experts believe, microchip power will double and costs will halve every eighteen months or so.

The computer has given birth to a prodigy-child – the Internet. A few decades ago, only a few government officials and university eggheads could access the Internet. Now, anyone with a small modem and a PC, notebook or hand-held computer can hook themselves into a vast web of online services.

132 *The Pioneer Spirit*

We can bank, shop, research, talk, play games, make phone calls, download music and watch movies or TV – all via the net. Internet terms are quickly finding their way into mainstream language. William Gibson was one of the first writers to spot the attraction computer games would hold for people around the world. He talked about an imaginary realm 'behind the screen', which, he said, people would treat as if it were a real place. He called it 'cyberspace' and, almost instantly, a new word was added to our dictionaries. Terms like 'information superhighway' and a host of others have since joined it.

The Good Stuff

It's not hard to see how all these developments in media technology have brought real benefits into our lives. Here are a few:

1. Democratization
Through the media, liberal democratic and human rights values are being made accessible to people living under repressive regimes. The 'world-wideness' of today's media has made it impossible for governments in nations like North Korea and China to isolate their people from democratic trends in other parts of the world. If, as many historians believe, the 1900s will be seen in posterity as the 'American Century', this will be due in no small part to the global impact of America's media.

2. Fast dissemination of news and information
It is popularly agreed in media circles that the Gulf War of 1991 made the reputation of CNN. Before that time, CNN had largely been a US news organisation, but afterwards it became a truly credible global outlet.

Jesus On the Airwaves

With the proliferation of specialist news outlets on TV, we have greater choice as to how we want to be informed. This also means that news sources must become more accountable. In a well-developed media market, no company is going to report something badly, when it can quickly be shown up by its competitors.

3. Greater individualization

TIME magazine commentator Walter Isaacson noted that 'Gutenberg's printing press . . . cut the cost of transmitting information by a factor of a thousand. That paved the way for the Reformation by allowing individuals to have their own Bibles, and for the progress of individual liberties, which became inevitable once information and ideas flowed freely. The transistor and the microchip have cut the cost of transmitting information by a factor of more than a million.'[3]

The printing press brought with it a whole new range of personal liberties that had been opposed by kings and bishops for centuries. In the same way, today's media have increased our sense of being in control of our lives.

4. Economic freedom and consumer choice

Through the proliferation of mass media, we are given quick and cheap access to the latest information on world money markets. That makes decision-making easier for both big companies and small investors alike.

The Internet also gives us ready access to a much broader range of information on what products and services are available. Of course, no amount of technology will prevent some people from being suckered into buying useless or poorly made products, but advertising means that we have more options.

134 *The Pioneer Spirit*

5. *More work and training for artists*

Radio, TV and film, have helped to develop the talents of many thousands of artists, including actors, directors, musicians, animators, set creators, fashion designers, writers and comics.

Each of these media relies heavily on highly trained, creative people working with specialized skills. For example, while it was once called the 'poor man's theatre', television now boasts its own movie industry. Movies made for TV are big business. They are normally cheaper to make than cinema films, yet they require their own peculiar skills. On TV, for example, there is more emphasis on the close-up shot, which is ideal for the small screen and, because budgets are smaller and release times shorter, design and scripting for TV require special abilities.

The Down Side

There are also some not-so-positive aspects of the electronic media explosion.

1. *The loss of word power*

In a world of growing alienation, the ability to negotiate, to share ideas and to work toward mutually beneficial goals is becoming more and more important.

Words are still our primary tools of communication. Most English-speaking people use only about four hundred words in everyday conversation. Yet, there are four hundred and fifty thousand useable words in the English language. We tend to use the same words repeatedly. If we could just learn a few new words each week, we would not only increase our knowledge but also our leadership ability.

Jesus On the Airwaves

Our reliance on picture-based communication, and our tendency to sacrifice interactive 'people time' for entertainment media, may reduce our skills in literacy and communication.

2. A loss of privacy

After the tragic death of Princess Diana, there was a furore about the role of the paparazzi. The whole sad affair left people asking serious questions. How much do we really want – or need – to know about the private life of a public figure? And how much of that information can really be gained in an ethical way? In this information-crazy, entertainment-addicted age, public figures often find themselves living in a media-built fishbowl.

However, the loss of privacy doesn't only affect the famous. Surrounded as we are by electronic credit card fraud, junk emails and the like, many of us lesser-known mortals are concerned about who is getting information about us. Sometimes, personal information, from addresses and buying preferences to medical histories, seems to be shooting across computer networks without our knowledge or consent.

3. The lowering of public standards

With the electronic media, it often seems that what was distasteful just yesterday is considered acceptable and even laudable today. Even politicians, so often loath to get involved in talk about morality, now acknowledge that public standards on public nudity, violence and pornography have fallen in recent times.

In 1999, two former American presidents, Carter and Ford, joined forces with celebrities and leading academics to call on Hollywood to reduce the exposure of children to what they called an increasingly toxic popular culture. Their open letter was motivated largely

136 *The Pioneer Spirit*

by the shootings at Littleton in Colorado, where two students killed thirteen people and then themselves. It suggested that there is a direct link between excessively violent and degrading entertainment and horrific new crimes emerging among young people. At the same time, President Clinton commissioned a study into the advertising of movies, music and video games to children. He called for a stricter enforcement of movie ratings.

Sadly, despite efforts like these, we will almost certainly see standards drop ever further. As so-called 'tolerance' grows in the community, so does moral entropy – our natural tendency to move toward the lowest moral denominator – unless we repent and reach out to God.

When accused of showing too graphic portrayals of violence or sex, media people will often respond with something like this: 'That's just what reality is like – we're only reflecting real life behaviours.' But how long can you go on *reflecting* a value system before you start *reinforcing* it – especially among the young and the vulnerable. You end up contributing to the sin by reminding people of how it's done.

One Australian study found that the average child spends eleven thousand hours at school. In the same period, he or she will watch around eighteen thousand murders as depicted on TV and in movies.[4] Links have also been established between media coverage of some murders and various copycat crimes. Experts know, too, that teenage suicides often occur in 'clusters'. These clusters, they say, are caused by imitation. Sensationalized or romanticized media coverage of one teenage suicide may fuel the suicidal tendencies of other teens.

Jesus On the Airwaves

4. Brain drain

In some ways, our infatuation with electronic media may cost us in our intellectual development. In 1979, Ayatollah Khomeini banned music on Iranian radio stations. He said that music 'stupefies the person listening to it and makes their brains inactive and frivolous.'[5] I certainly don't agree with that statement or with the attitudes behind it.

Music is one of the greatest of all God's gifts to the human soul. I do think, though, that repetition of the same trite inconsequential music or media messages day after day can inoculate people against using their minds to the full. If you don't believe it, spend an hour listening to muzak in a supermarket or riding up in an elevator – see what that does to your brain cells!

5. Spirit drain

By giving so much of our time to the media, we've also made sacrifices in our spiritual make-up. Malcolm Muggeridge was a key figure in the British media for a number of decades. He wrote as a correspondent in World War II, published books and plays and became an integral part of the development of TV journalism in the UK. He was something of a prophetic voice through newspapers, magazines and television. He used wit and a very sharp mind to get to the root of complex issues and personalities.

Muggeridge recognized early on that our western culture was changing from a verbal to a visual one. Part of the downside of this, he felt, is that people tend to believe in the truthfulness of the images they see in the media. He wrote: 'the camera cannot lie, they assure themselves, and when it does, [they] succumb to its falsehoods.'[6]

Muggeridge also bemoaned what he saw as the

138 *The Pioneer Spirit*

reduction of our ability to see with spiritual eyes, and the growing cult of scientific rationalism that makes a god of looking for the material 'facts' and keeps spiritual reality at bay. He wrote: 'Prostrating themselves before facts, appealing to facts for guidance in time of trouble, [people] credit them with a validity they do not possess, and lay themselves open to deceptions greater than any the imagination can practise.'[7]

Some truths can only be seen with the eye of the spirit; some aspects of reality can only be experienced through the exercise of conscience and faith. To paraphrase Deuteronomy 8:3, 'Man does not live, really live, by what he sees alone, but by believing through faith in what he does not see.'

6. The 'Houdini' age

With our reliance on media has come a greater capacity for escapism. For most people today, entertainment is more than an interesting sideline – it's a central part of their lives. We have, as one writer suggested, invented the sixth basic human need. To the need for food, shelter and so on, we have added the need for novelty. We need to be entertained.

We sometimes find it more rewarding to watch another life, even an imaginary one, played out on a screen than to enjoy our own lives to the full. We find it less stressful to experience life's ups and downs vicariously, through someone else's story. Real living, though, is not about the absence of tension or problems, but the ability to face up to and overcome the pressure.

7. Haves and have-nots

Despite the falling costs of some equipment, it's still true that only the world's middle classes and wealthy have access to the full benefits of the media. The Internet is accessible to just a fraction of the world's population. If

Jesus On the Airwaves

you lived in Bangladesh, you would need to save your wages for eight months to pay for a basic PC.

In some areas, ownership of a TV is still rare. Access to media has become yet another barrier between the world's haves and have-nots. Of course, the have-nots are the ones who really need the education opportunities the media can provide.

8. Elevation of celebrity over achievement

'A celebrity,' said one wit, 'is a person who is known for his well-knownness.'

Once upon a time, celebrities were people whom we celebrated because they had actually done something notable or heroic with their lives. Nowadays, people are famous just because they can afford to pay image consultants to *make* them famous.

Many people hang on every word uttered by movie and music stars. It's as if their fame has given them insight into some great, unfathomable wisdom – when, in fact, they often prove by their lifestyles that they don't have a clue! For example, we often hear stars asked what they think it takes to build a great relationship. Sometimes, we put the question to people who have experienced a string of relationship breakdowns. Why ask the questions of people who obviously don't know the answers? Celebrity is not a guarantee of wisdom.

9. Loss in interpersonal relationships

Shopping from the comfort of home, chatting on the net and sofa-surfing through the TV channels, are all contributing to a decrease in the ability of some people to relate to others, face-to-face. Today, our social and family-building skills are under attack while we quietly let the TV glow wash over us. We acquiesce to a life that involves the minimum number of real people.

140 *The Pioneer Spirit*

I'm not arguing that the media influence in our lives is all bad. The fact remains though, that these areas of loss are hardly ever addressed and unless we do face up to them, we are cheating our families and ourselves. Producers and presenters working in the media need to offer programmes that affect positive change in these areas. As media users, we must discipline our habits so that we keep the influence of media in its proper place, as our servant rather than our master.

Jesus on the Box

Christians see the electronic media as amoral tools that have to be turned to some end, for good or ill. To pioneer Christians, the electronic media represent huge opportunities for creative, positive influence on the world around them. Pioneer Christians are not paranoid about the dangers of electronic media. Sure, they can see the dangers, but they're committed to redeeming media as tools that can be turned to a good end.

The apostle Paul said something that's relevant here:

Be very careful, then, how you live – not as unwise but as wise, making the most of every opportunity, because the days are evil. (Ephesians 5:15–16)

The King James Version of that verse says we should be 'redeeming the time because the days are evil.' In media work we talk about 'airtime'. Christians need to redeem the airtime, to reclaim the electronic media as means of communication for God's use.

Christians should not be afraid of media influence. In fact, Christian leaders have often been among the first people to recognize the real potential of media.

Jesus On the Airwaves 141

In the US, Christian preachers were among the first to see the potential of networked radio stations. They raised the money and produced the programmes that filled many hours of broadcast time, helping radio broadcasting to become a truly 'coast-to-coast' phenomenon. In many of these programmes, the standards of production were very high, enabling technicians to develop their skills.

Renowned American evangelist Billy Graham has preached 'live' to more people than perhaps anyone else in history. However, the Graham organisation has also been quick to see, use and promote emerging media through the years. It was, for example, among the first organisations to film large public events and distribute them around the world. Films of Billy Graham meetings have been seen by millions of people. The Graham organisation also produced a number of dramas and documentaries, for TV and cinema.

Billy Graham was also one of the first to see and utilize the full potential of satellite TV. Long before CNN became a household name, local churches were hooking up local satellite feeds to witness Graham's meetings. Many people came to Christ in local community halls. These hook-ups represented a huge investment of manpower and money, and showed what could be done with television if people in many places were willing to network their skills.

Renowned preacher Oral Roberts was another minister who invested time and money in developing media for outreach and mission. He founded a media wing in his ministry that produced movies and opened the way for some of the first presentations of the gospel on network TV. Today, that media group functions as a highly effective advertising agency. It still aims to take Christian values to the widest possible audience.

Canada's Crossroads network is now among one of the most respected media organisations in North America.

142 *The Pioneer Spirit*

Its programmes present positive and empathic Christian responses to everyday issues and concerns and its counselling services help thousands of people to deal with everyday problems, both spiritual and practical.

Of course, Christians outside of North America have also been influential in the development of media. In Britain, for example, a committed Scottish Christian, Lord Reith, led the BBC for many years. Reith saw TV as a means of encouraging righteousness in society and promoting Christian values.

In Scandinavia, Christian apostles like Lewi Pethrus pioneered the use of radio and TV to share the faith. At one point, when the government threatened to close down his radio station, Pethrus boldly declared that if they did, he'd simply buy a ship and broadcast to the mainland from there. That kind of ingenuity shows a real understanding of the power of electronic media, long before they were as powerful as they are today.

Staying in Touch

The church of today needs this same foresight when it comes to fast-developing media like computer gaming and computer animation.

Today, many churches around the world are dedicating considerable financial resources to developing cutting-edge media ministries. Some larger churches own TV stations and even networks. Wherever churches are having an impact through media, it is because their leaders have received a real mandate from God. They have made media more than an appendix to an existing vision. Media has become a central part of their planning.

In the days ahead, Christian leaders, artists and ministries will need to stay in touch with emerging media

Jesus On the Airwaves

technologies and techniques. Changes are occurring at an amazing rate. Once we allow ourselves to get just a couple of paces behind the latest trends, we will find ourselves frozen out of new opportunities.

Sorgaard observes that, 'Change in methods and media is necessary if we are to use our gifts to the fullest, and turn our attention from the medium to the person. A method-bound movement cannot become an effective world movement, but it will soon be relegated to the outdated and the outworn.'[8]

If the battle between light and darkness is fought anywhere, it is fought in the media arena. If Christians allow themselves to drop out of the media loop, they may never be allowed back in again.

When it comes to media, we need to commit ourselves to forward thinking and bold, strategic planning. Nothing in the media happens purely by accident. We must be praying and planning for success. We must focus on inventing media packages that meet people's needs. We must pioneer positive new approaches to sharing the gospel via the media.

1. Viggo Sorgaard, *Media in Church and Mission: Communicating the Gospel* (William Carey Library, 1993), p. 188
2. Gregory Wolfe, *Malcolm Muggeridge, a Biography*, (Hodder and Stoughton, 1995), p. 277
3. Walter Isaacson, 'Our Century and the Next One', (*TIME*, April 13, 1998)
4. Susan Hocking, 'Control the television and you control young minds', (*The Mail on Sunday*, Sept. 11, 1988)
5. Quoted Sorgaard, Op. Cit., p.151
6. Gregory Wolfe, Op. Cit., p.178
7. Ibid. p.178
8. Viggo Sorgaard, Op. Cit., p. 21

9

Beyond Church-on-TV

'Darling, can you please wash the car today?'

'Hey, did you read this bit in the newspaper this morning? It's unbelievable . . .'

'Did you hear what I said, honey?'

'I mean, listen to this . . .'

'I said . . . can you please wash the car today?'

'It says here that the average child only has around fifteen minutes of meaningful interaction with a parent each week!'

'Only, we've got to go to my mother's tomorrow, and the car's filthy.'

'Do you think that's true? If it is, well, I'm not surprised the nation's in trouble.'

'You know how mum hates mess – and we've got to drive her to the supermarket, remember.'

'I mean, what kind of family is it where people don't ever really talk to each other? Incredible . . .'

Communication is much more than one person getting something off his or her chest. Real communication is a two-way street. 'Nothing is taught,' wrote one teacher, 'until something is learned.'

Beyond Church-on-TV 145

What is the measure of good communication? Is it whether people laugh at your jokes or cry when you tell them a sad story? None of the above. You can only say that you've succeeded in the communication process when people are acting on what you've said – and producing something fruitful as a result.

Many of us use what social researcher Hugh MacKay has called 'The Injection Method' of communication. We tend to think that if we can just find the right words (the 'medicine') and put them into the right medium (the 'syringe'), we can simply 'inject' ideas into the mind of another person. This is based on two very wrong assumptions:

1. That people are blank slates who are just waiting to receive my message; that they have nothing else on their minds.
2. That my words have meanings in and of themselves.

People do not come into the communication process as blank slates. They bring with them the heritage – or baggage – of their past and present experiences. When I seek to share something with other human beings, my words have no meaning in themselves. The hearers – who measure my words against the backdrop of their education, background, hopes and concerns – ascribe meaning to my words. It's not what my words do to the hearers that counts, but what the hearers do with my words. Unless I've taken the time to understand my audience, my words will fall on uncomprehending ears.

I suppose the medium of communication most associated with the church is preaching. Say that word these days and most people conjure up visions of someone standing behind a lofty pulpit, looking down their nose at them and telling them things they neither want nor need to hear. But that's not the Bible's view of

146 The Pioneer Spirit

preaching. In fact, the New Testament word that's most often translated 'preaching' is the Greek word *kerusso*. It literally means communicating and sharing ideas.

We take the English word 'communication' from the Latin root *communer*, which simply means 'to share'. In his ground-breaking book, *SoulTsunami*, Leonard Sweet reminds us that the word communication means 'to bring together in one'.[1]

To communicate is to bring people together, around ideas. Why was President John F. Kennedy a great communicator? Because he could get people to think about what they could do for their country, rather than what it could do for them. Why was Martin Luther King so influential? Because he knew how to rally people around a dream that he expressed so eloquently, forcefully, even poetically, in words. Why was Winston Churchill so successful in rallying the people of London and Britain for war? Because, as President Kennedy put it, he 'took words and sent them into battle'.

These were all great communicators. Yet, they pale when placed beside Jesus Christ. His words have reverberated down through the centuries and millennia to touch us in ways that no other words have ever done. We've never heard a recording of Jesus' voice. We don't know what his accent sounded like. We have no idea how deep or high his voice was. Yet, so great was the force of his personality that we can almost hear him speak every time we read the gospels.

So deeply were Jesus' words seared into the minds of his followers, that they remembered them word-for-word for decades, until the time came to commit them to paper. The influence of Christ in history is in no small part due to his uncanny ability to connect with his audience – both then and now. As God incarnate, Jesus is our proof that God is the supreme communicator.

Beyond Church-on-TV

Ultimately, all communication is rooted in the nature of God. According to the Bible, God exists as a Trinity – three persons in one essence.[2] The Father communicates with the Son, the Son with the Holy Spirit, and the Holy Spirit with the Father. There's a constant flow of communication within the Godhead, at a level we can't even begin to imagine.

God loves to reveal himself to human beings. From the very beginning of the Bible record, God has been uncovering to men and women his nature and his character. He longs to show us what he is like, in a way that we can understand. He makes the transcendent immanent.

Communication is central to who God is. He is love and love, by its very nature, seeks to reveal itself.[3] Communication is also central to who *we* are because we are made in God's image. Like God, we ache to reveal our innermost thoughts and dreams to others.

Jesus last command was that we communicate – to the world.

'Go into all the world and preach the good news to all creation'. (Mark 16:15)

That's a command tailor-made for a media generation. In our age, for the first time in history, we are able to communicate over huge spaces with comparatively little cost – and sometimes without even leaving home.

For a Christian seeking to have influence through the media, the big question has to be this: What would Jesus do? If Jesus were on TV, or working on the Internet, or making a movie, what would be the hallmarks of his work? I believe we can find in Jesus' life some powerful principles to guide us toward effective communication in the media.

Wearing Your Faith . . .

When the Levis Jeans Company want to sell you their product, they don't drape a pair of jeans over a clothes hanger and say, 'Look at these great jeans – wouldn't they look good on you?' They take their jeans and hang them on gorgeous models: people who look like they were born in these jeans, so that they fit them like a glove. The advertisers are selling you much more than jeans; they're offering you a concept and selling you a lifestyle.

The advertisement says to you, 'This is how these jeans will change your life.' Because the model looks confident, you can expect to be confident. Because the model has cool friends, you can expect to have cool friends. All you need to do is buy the jeans.

What are the advertisers doing? They're modelling a new way of life. They're 'incarnating' their version of reality, showing you what a difference it could make in your world.

Advertising works well because we love to see a truth modelled for us. We're wired that way. God created in us a hunger to see truth demonstrated, because that's how he reveals himself to us – through incarnation. God modelled his vision of humanity for us, in the form of his son, Jesus. When we look at the life of Christ, we see God 'wearing' human form. We can see how God's character relates to our own experience.

In a similar way, God calls every Christian to incarnate his truth, to model his message before the world. This is our calling: to reveal how our faith in God makes a difference to everyday concerns and needs. That's the beauty of electronic media: they provide a canvas so that we can paint narrative pictures, which represent truth in an emotionally captivating way. Media can help us incarnate Jesus' love and power.

Beyond Church-on-TV

There can be no denying the power of images and stories. They touch us at a deep level that systematic teaching or essays on truth cannot reach. G. K. Chesterton said that he distrusted anything that could not be represented in stories or coloured pictures. Aristotle claimed that the soul never thinks without a mental picture and Carl Jung taught that images are bridges thrown towards an invisible shore.

God has always used visual images to express his plans for his people. He painted Noah a rainbow and pointed Abraham to the countless stars in the night sky.[4] Moses was given a bush on fire and Jacob saw a ladder leading into heaven.[5] When Jesus died, and the old covenant ended, God made sure we would see the significance by tearing the temple curtain from top to bottom.[6]

The greatest exponent of metaphors and animated pictures was Jesus himself. I often wonder what Jesus would have done with animation. He was so skilled at creating vivid images filled with action and intrigue. Leonard Sweet says, 'The communication style of Jesus was a narrative style . . . [It was] dominated by mental pictures that conveyed more than words. Jesus taught in parables, analogies, figures of speech and startling metaphors to stir the sediment of people's hearts and open their eyes to the deeper meanings of life.'[7]

Modern media are at their best when they're used to present parables that incarnate truth. They are less effective when used to pump out systematic, polemic statements of truth. There is definitely a place for church-on-TV programmes but they don't represent the best use of this parabolic, story-telling medium. With a little creative thinking, we can break out of our sermonising mould and present truth in ways that draw people into the process. We can open people's lives to change.

150 *The Pioneer Spirit*

The goal of all incarnation – or modelling – is to fit the message into the life-frame of the audience. That requires effort. It requires that we are listening. Listening is the foundation to all great communication. Great communication is receptor-oriented: it does not focus on the giver, but seeks to meet the need of the receiver.

Every trained counsellor knows the importance of empathic responding. Professional counsellors are trained to interact with others so that they not only hear what people are saying; they also experience what people are feeling. Through empathic responding, the counsellor tries to see the world through the other person's eyes, to get inside his or her 'reality bubble' for a while. Once there, the counsellor is more aware of possible solutions.

This kind of interactive listening is also important when it comes to media communication. We can't meet any need, or offer any worthwhile service, unless we know the felt needs of our audience.

Watching us on TV, reading us on the web or listening to us on the radio, people can tell if we've been interacting with the real world. They can tell if we're in touch with the same kinds of situations that they face. All that is made clear by the style of our presentation and by the substance of what we're saying.

That's why, for anyone who's serious about sharing the gospel through media, research is the indispensable first step. Research helps us in several ways:

1. Research helps us to define our objective and our audience

Ask many Christian leaders, 'Who do you want to reach with your TV programme or your website?' and you'll get the following response: 'Everybody'.

That sounds very inclusive and all, but the fact is that media audiences are highly segmented these days.

Beyond Church-on-TV 151

There's a veritable army of consultants working in media today who do nothing more than study and advise on demographics. Media companies also use focus groups to sharpen their appeal to a particular audience. People of different age groups enjoy different types of programming – and they watch or listen at different times of the day. People also respond differently to programmes on the basis of their social, ethnic and economic environment. Producers work *with* the reality of a segmented audience, deliberately focussing their resources on specific age and interest groups.

Have you ever seen a person in a wheelchair approach the entrance to a building that has no access ramp? The look on his or her face is one of sheer frustration and anger. It's as if someone has painted a huge sign on the door saying, 'Physically disabled people, stay out!'

If we're not careful, Christian initiatives can turn out like that. Our style of presentation and the substance of what we say can seem totally irrelevant to people outside of the church. Many people in our world are attracted to Jesus, while finding the church difficult to relate to. They come to the church's door in need, but find no 'access ramps'. There are no points of connection between what the church is saying or doing and their situation. So, they turn away in frustration.

Media programming can provide the access ramps. It can build bridges of understanding and trust – if we will base our approach on people's needs, instead of our own interests.

2. Research reveals perceived needs
As Christians, we may feel that what we have to offer is universal in its appeal. But universal truth must be applied in focussed ways, to specific needs.

From a Christian perspective, there is often a difference

150   *The Pioneer Spirit*

between a person's 'perceived' needs and their 'real' needs. The latter may be spiritual. There is, after all, only so much that can be done to help someone who is out of relationship with God. Our ultimate goal as Christians is to reconcile people to God.[8]

Not everyone we meet, however, will see his or her spiritual condition in the way that we might. So, it's important for us to start where people feel they are right now. The most pressing need, as they perceive it, may be repairing a struggling marriage, or dealing with a problem child, or getting out of debt. We need to bring God's truth into that practical situation, in the hope that we can earn their trust and help them on a spiritual level.

Jesus did this with the woman at the well, in John chapter 4. He started the conversation at the point of the woman's perceived need – the need for water. Then, within a short while, he helped her to see that what she really needed was something even more life-giving – spiritual water. The conversation that followed had a profound impact on this lonely woman. It changed her life *and* the lives of half the people in her village.[9]

Many Christian leaders approach the media in the wrong way. They blunder straight into a spiritual message, without first developing the trust and respect of their audience. Because they don't talk about the felt needs of the audience, they're never given the chance to address spiritual needs. People simply turn them off!

3. Research identifies our resources

In any media project, the basic resources are people, organisation, facilities and funds. In a production team, we need to consider this question: what resources are available for the project at hand?

If the project is too big for our own organisation to handle alone, or if it would benefit from outside

Beyond Church-on-TV 153

assistance, we'll need to find gifted people in other, like-minded groups with whom we can work. That will require that we clearly define some roles. Every person will need a job description, including clear lines of accountability. All team members need to know who is above them in the chain of command and who is available to help when they have a problem.

In these days of diversification and specialisation, very successful media projects are usually the product of strong alliances. They rely on partnerships between different producers, between producers and financiers and between producers and broadcasters – to name a few. The same will apply in church-based media work. I'm sure there are many potentially great media projects that will never see the light of day simply because organisations are not willing to pool their resources or to rely on outside help.

4. Research helps us to analyse media and methods

Different media are received differently by various people groups. Teenagers and young adults, for example, listen to FM radio and watch MTV more than most older people. Shift workers watch TV during the day, and children have special viewing times after school.

We need to identify which media and which times are most attractive to the groups we want to reach. In some cases, of course, our choices are limited. We may not have the money to present our programmes where we'd ultimately like to. Sometimes, we just have to make the best of available opportunities, tailoring our presentation to suit the audience, instead of imposing our ideal on an unwilling public.

154   *The Pioneer Spirit*

5. *Research helps us to measure and evaluate our performance*

Research helps us to forecast results before we launch a project. It helps us to make projections about what we are likely to achieve – in terms of audience size, age and so on. Consequently, we can set up follow-up systems to work with people who want to know more.

In the end, the same kind of research can help us to measure our effectiveness against our goals. If we are to be good stewards of God-given resources, we'll need to hold ourselves to account, by continually asking some key questions. Are we reaching our objectives? Have we impacted the age group we set out to attract? Have we been able to take people through a process of growth; have we led them any closer to real discipleship? Could we be using our resources more effectively? Are there lessons we might learn to help us improve our performance?

These are all testing questions, but unless we have the courage and the skills to face them, we'll waste precious time and resources. We'll end up making programmes that people don't want to see or hear.

The other benefit of evaluation, of course, is that it can give us the kind of feedback we need to raise financial sponsorships. People with the money to invest in media projects are not usually impressed with vague, unproven ideas or with producers who are not planning for maximum results.

For a Christian communicator or organisation, research doesn't replace the direct guidance of God's Holy Spirit – far from it. We can't do anything of eternal worth without the agency of Christ's love and power. However, research can show us where we *need* God's guidance. It can remove distractions from our path and help to slim down the available options, so that we're

Beyond Church-on-TV

praying and working toward a much more focussed objective.

Understanding the Medium

The second key to great media communication is a grasp of the medium.

'The medium,' said Marshall McLuhan, 'is the message.' The way we say something speaks as loudly about the message as the content itself. We need to understand the media we use and how they are received by the audience or we may end up sending out the wrong signals.

Aside from public speaking, the media I use most are writing and television. Whilst the church has traditionally produced some first-class writers, TV is a medium that we've been slow to understand. For that reason, I'd like to use television as an example of what we should and should not do with electronic media in general. You can apply any of the principles that follow to any medium.

TV is not at its best when it is used as a pulpit. There is a place for church-on-TV programmes, but I don't think they represent the best use of the medium.

Before I go any further, though, let me say this. I am committed to the media, but I am also a preacher. Without doubt, anointed preaching is still one of the most potent forms of communication known to man. In fact, one of the tragedies of recent western history is that we've removed the arts from the church, and preaching from the community.

Great preaching is polemic. That's its power: it presents truth in a black-and-white manner, calling for change in line with the word of God. Preaching can

156 *The Pioneer Spirit*

inspire, challenge and bring revelation. We should appreciate the beauty of fine preaching and respect the craftsmanship of those who do it well.

However, we need to see the weaknesses of preaching as well as its strengths. When it comes to electronic media, preaching has some real limitations. We must never let the method of communication be our primary concern, so that we focus more on means than on ends. We must always look toward the end goal, which is changing people's lives.

We need to remember four things if we're to make the best use of electronic media such as television:

1. Electronic media are interactive and team-oriented
Church-on-TV often fails to address the interactive nature of TV. Pulpit preaching is, by nature, a one-way communication medium. Good television, however, is a forum, a marketplace where ideas are presented for consideration. The picture Christian leaders need to fix in their minds is that of Paul sharing his convictions with 'outsiders' on Mars Hill, rather than Paul teaching the converted at Ephesus.[10]

In a bygone age, the church in a town was the centre for the dissemination of news and opinions. It was the core of much of the social interaction and the shaper of the moral and ethical standards of the community. In most of the western world, all that changed a long time ago. For many people, the church has become just another service industry. If they want groceries, they go to the supermarket. If they need petrol, they head for the gas station. If they need religion, then they go to church.

The bottom line is this: Christian leaders can no longer expect to be heard just because *they* believe they're speaking for God. Christian preachers are competing with the thousands of other messages people receive

Beyond Church-on-TV 157

every day. People need to be convinced that what we have to say is going to benefit them. We must earn the right to be heard and we must do it in a way that says, 'I respect *your* power in this process.'

Yet, many Christian leaders who work on TV are producing programmes that seem to say, 'You should listen to me, because I have a big Bible, a large church and a nice pulpit.' TV can mask a person's character, but it can also magnify character flaws. One trait the camera is quick to reveal is arrogance. Many Christian leaders seem to forget that when people watch us on TV, they're actually inviting us into their homes. *We are on their turf, not our own.*

Now, I don't know about you, but when people call on me at home, I don't expect them to bring a pulpit or to stand in my living room and deliver long and windy monologues. I certainly wouldn't expect a guest to talk *at* me for half an hour and then try to take money from me!

This is my home. I deserve some consideration, some respect. When people visit me, I want us to have dialogue and interesting interaction, with no barriers between us.

When it comes to media like TV, we may have the very best intentions in the world. But if we don't understand the media we use, the audience may look on our presentation as just another soapbox or propaganda vehicle. That does not make for attractive television. Worse still, we can look like people who're scared to stop talking in case others cut in with something we don't like. It can seem that we're afraid of the ideas of others. In fact, the church has nothing to fear from the truth. All truth, as C. S. Lewis put it, is God's truth. We are more of a threat to false ideas than they are to us! We welcome truth with open arms, because truth sets people free.[11]

Great television is also a team effort. Many of today's highest rating comedy and drama series feature actors

158 *The Pioneer Spirit*

working in ensembles. Top news and variety programmes sometimes use two hosts instead of one. Even where there is one 'star', you'll often find behind-the-scenes team members being included in the on-screen fun. It's as if the producers have taken the skeleton, the frame of a great building and placed it on the outside. They've taken the parts that are normally hidden from view and revealed them for all to see.

What does teamwork like this do for a programme? For one thing, it increases a programme's power to connect with an audience. Seeing different faces on screen makes audience members feel that they can connect. If they don't relate to one character or presenter, they'll pick up on another.

Getting the team involved also says to the audience, 'This thing is bigger than one guy or one woman. There's a place for you in all of this. You, the viewer, are an extension of our team.'

The problem with many church-on-TV programmes is that they tend to revolve around just one person for most of the time. Consequently, there are fewer 'connection points' for the audience. (Besides, since when do we spend half an hour or more in real life looking at just one face?)

On-screen teamwork can make a programme seem more down-to-earth, too. It says, in an indirect way, 'We don't take anyone – especially ourselves – too seriously.' Some preaching programmes come across as being preoccupied with their own importance. They seem to be saying, 'This preacher is not like average people. He's got all the answers. If you don't hear what they have to say you're missing everything that's good on TV!'

If we don't work to understand the medium, what we might think is a powerful presentation can actually come across as a stern, self-righteous lecture. One thing is certain: lectures make for terrible television.

Beyond Church-on-TV 159

Of course, teamwork goes beyond what the audience sees on the screen. When they see a quality programme of any kind, people know that there's a team working off-camera. The production values alone suggest that all kinds of skilled people are giving their best for the project.

Promoting that kind of team-based excellence is something that should come naturally for the church. After all, the church is the Body of Christ, a living organism in which each individual member invests his or her gifts for the common good.[12] TV production gives us a great opportunity to see the Body at work, as it calls upon many kinds of gifts: set construction, videography, music, fashion design, editing, animation, sound and lighting, financing and much more.

2. *The dynamics of TV are different to those of the stage*
In some ways, the difference between TV and live preaching is much the same as that between TV and live theatre.

Stage plays rarely work well when shot as live action for TV. Plays usually need to be re-written, or at least directed in a completely new way for the screen. The dynamics, movements and pace are all different on stage.

In most theatres, audience members are seated in a large room, with each one being a long way from the action on stage. Stage performers need to project, to emphasize their actions and their voices so that people can pick up the subtleties of the performance.

That distance between audience and performer is not an issue with TV – or, at least, not in the same way. What actors do on stage needs to be toned down for television's smaller viewing area and its more intimate appeal.

Techniques that make a great stage performance will not necessarily make for good television. In the same

160 *The Pioneer Spirit*

way, preaching that's powerful in church will not necessarily carry the same weight on TV.

Some preachers tone down a 'live' message too much for the benefit of TV. Instead of allowing the Holy Spirit to move them and the church, they stand transfixed behind a pulpit as if their feet were set in concrete and their hands handcuffed behind their backs. There's no passion or force in their ministry. There's no spiritual energy or authority imparted to the people.

Conversely, some TV preachers wave their hands about, shout at the tops of their voices and walk up and down on screen like a caged lion. All this might be captivating in church, but it seems threatening – sometimes, even comical – on TV.

Passion is about bringing the entire force of your personality and the full range of your creativity to bear on whatever task is before you. It is not about histrionics and hype.

Here's the bottom line. Preaching in church is preaching in church. Making TV is making TV. We *should* fully explore the benefits of preaching, but we must develop the strengths of TV as something separate. We need to make TV programmes *for* TV, exploring all of the creative opportunities the medium has to offer us.

Christians often have an either/or mentality when it comes to evangelism and entertainment. Either a project is sharing Christ or it is entertaining, but never both. What a travesty! How can we accept that people find us boring when we're representing the most captivating man who ever lived?

3. Church-on-TV has become all that people expect from Christians!

Of course, I would rather have church-on-TV programmes than have no Christian presence in the media at

Beyond Church-on-TV

all. It is good, as the apostle Paul wrote, that the message of Christ is being exalted even if we don't totally approve of the messenger.[13] However, we need to redress the imbalance that currently exists. Church-on-TV is the only form of Christian-based programming many people know – and it has no influence in their day-to-day lives.

Perhaps the biggest enemy of all communication is predictability. When people *think* they know what's coming next, they tune out. A joke is never as funny the second time around, and most of us don't read a particular novel more than once. Predictability is a turn-off.

Many people think they know all about what Christians believe and the way Christians act. So they stop listening to us, because they think we have nothing new to say to them. Pulpits and preaching are what many people have come to *expect* of the church, so when they see them on TV their first impulse is to tune out. Before we've had a chance to prove otherwise, they've rejected what we say as irrelevant. Our style has cut them off from the substance of our message.

If we're going to present Jesus through the media, we must first break down people's preconceived ideas about Christian faith. We won't do that by coming up with programmes that *support* those stereotypes.

The best TV programmes are interesting, colourful, entertaining, informative and emotionally involving, all at the same time. Electronic media allow us to be innovative and adventurous, to present a face of Christianity that few people know exists. Creative use of media lets us take people by surprise.

4. TV is about sowing, not just reaping

At times in the church, we've forgotten that evangelism and disciple-making are processes, not events. They both take time and each of them relies upon the other. I

162 *The Pioneer Spirit*

suspect that part of the reason for our bias in favour of church-on-TV programmes is that we've lost sight of the importance of sowing.

Sowing is not as glamorous as reaping. It doesn't usually attract the same financial support, either. Yet, the better prepared the soil of a human heart is, the more receptive it will be to the gospel. If our sowing is half-hearted or under-resourced, how can we hope to see a good harvest?

Our ultimate goal is always to lead people towards a personal commitment to Christ, but media like television offer us so many wonderful opportunities to sow the seeds of Christian values, a biblical world-view and the salvation message. Sometimes, we insult people's intelligence. We assume that unless we cut everything up into small pieces, they won't be able to digest the truth!

Can preaching programmes work? Yes, in certain circumstances they're just the kind of medicine people need. But what doctor will prescribe the same medication for *every* complaint? We need to have more than one bottle in our media medicine cabinet.

The best of our preaching programmes would have a far bigger impact if they came on the back of other, more inventive forms of programming. If church-on-TV is to reap a harvest, we need to explore other forms of production as means of placing the seed. More sowing will bring greater reaping.

Honest to God!

Listening to people and understanding the media: these are two great keys to the creative use of electronic media. I suppose, though, that the greatest of all the allies we can call upon in communication is honesty.

Beyond Church-on-TV 163

We live in the age of 'spin'. Politicians and other public figures employ people to put their decisions and actions in the best possible light for public consumption. Media experts teach business leaders and public servants how to present the right face on TV. Spin-doctors and image consultants try to maximize their clients' standing in opinion polls.

Amidst all the 'spinning' and 'image-tuning', people find transparency and straightforwardness very refreshing. When Billy Joel sang about honesty, he said it is 'such a lonely word'. Sadly, people almost expect to be manipulated by the media. So much so that, when they're confronted with media figures who seem less concerned with slickness and more interested in being real, it can come as a very pleasant surprise.

In the media, integrity can be like the punchline to a joke: because it's what you least expect, it gets a great response.

In relationships, vulnerability breaks down barriers. All human relationships are based on transparency. The higher the degree of openness between people, the deeper will be their friendship. The more people reveal of themselves, the more they risk possible rejection, the greater is the trust they develop.

Trust is the foundation stone for all great media communication, just as it is in all good friendships. The best media communicators are people who audiences feel they know. When a media figure is thought of as a friend, a bridge of trust exists between him or her and the audience – a connection that's not easily destroyed. Of course, the friendship is an artificial one – even the audience knows that. Nevertheless, the confidence is real. It is a valuable commodity and it must never be manipulated or abused. It gives the media presenter a level of influence that he or she must respect.

164 *The Pioneer Spirit*

In the media, as in life, trust can come only as we take the risk of revealing our inner selves. Honesty begins with putting off artifice and being real. That's a challenge, of course, when it comes to appearing in the media. Media work has so much to do with appearances.

In real life, most of us will put on a 'public face' and a more private one depending on whom we are with. Our more intimate, private front is usually reserved for close friends. When we are in less familiar surroundings, we tend to be more circumspect and less relaxed and transparent. Most of us also tend to sound different when speaking to a camera than we do when talking to friends. On camera, as in any public setting, we put on our best face.

It's natural for us to want to look and sound our best for strangers. There's nothing wrong with that. In working with the media, though, we must avoid manipulating people's natural desire to believe in us. We shouldn't set out with the deliberate intention of deceiving people, of having them believe we're something that we're not.

It's OK to show your 'best side' in the media, provided it is *your* best side and not one that you've invented or borrowed. Acting is fine – as long as people *know* you're acting. After all, we serve a God who looks not on the outward appearance but on the heart.[14] A carefully-sculpted image does not fool or impress him.

If we can avoid being infatuated with the electronic media; if we can keep our integrity intact, we can redeem and transform them by our faith in Christ and invent new models for programming.

If we can also steer clear of the fame game and build our sense of identity on the word of God, we can reveal an authenticity the world hungers for.

If we can keep one goal before us – making God's

Beyond Church-on-TV 165

name great – we will truly meet human needs.

If we can do all of the above, we will offer the world something it has rarely seen – a Christianity that is both relevant *and* prophetic. Then, we will pioneer a new kind of media.

1. Leonard I. Sweet, *SoulTsunami* (Zondervan Publishing House, 1999), p. 201
2. Matthew 28:19
3. 1 John 4:8
4. Genesis 9:13–14; 15:5
5. Exodus 3:2; Genesis 28:12
6. Mark 15:38
7. Leonard I. Sweet, Op. Cit., p. 203
8. 2 Corinthians 5:20
9. John 4:1–24
10. Cf. Acts 17:16–34 and 19:9
11. John 8:32
12. 1 Corinthians 12:27
13. Philippians 1:15–18
14. 1 Samuel 16:7

I hope you've enjoyed this book, and that it's inspired you to think more strategically, live more passionately and release all of your God-given creativity!

I passionately believe that YOU can make a huge difference to people in this often confused post-modern age. So, I've written a special worksheet to help you discover how you can use YOUR unique gifts to redesign the future and make God famous.

It's filled with practical ideas, backed up with Bible guides.

You can get your personal copy of the worksheet by visiting the special 'Readers Only' section of our website:

www.malfletcher.com/tps/

It is time to re-dig those wells and release again the pioneer spirit.

Keep making God famous!

Mal Fletcher

About the Author

Mal Fletcher is committed to one thing above all else: Making God Famous!

Mal is a respected Christian pioneer and leader, a TV producer and presenter, and an internationally acclaimed speaker. In his unique and challenging style, he is explaining the Christian message to secular cultures via the media, outreach events and training conferences around the world. He is also equipping church leaders to relate the gospel to contemporary cultures.

His TV programme, *EDGES™ with Mal Fletcher*, can now be seen in over 210 countries, on Christian and major secular networks. *EDGES* is a colourful, fast-paced TV programme that takes a very different look at the social issues shaping the values of today's world and the lifestyles of tomorrow. It offers a Christian response to major social, moral and lifestyle issues. Issues covered include: terrorism, euthanasia, civil disobedience, robotics, witchcraft and more. These programmes are breaking new ground by bridging the gap between Christian production and secular broadcasters. The programmes also have a growing audience online at www.edges.tv.

Mal is the founder and executive director of *Next Wave*

168 *The Pioneer Spirit*

International™, a mission to contemporary cultures, with a special focus on Europe. Through this rapidly expanding mission, he and his team are not only reaching the unchurched via city-wide events, the Internet, TV and more; they are also equipping church and business leaders in the skills of contemporary leadership. The *MasterClasses* on communication, generations and leadership attract leaders from several nations.

Mal also is the pioneer and leader of the *Strategic Leadership Consultation* and *EYE* leadership networks across Europe. These annual network meetings bring together two generations of key apostolic Christian leaders in Europe for strategic planning and prayer. They have become 'must-attend' meetings for many of Europe's most successful church network leaders.

Mal's books on cultural and leadership issues have been translated into several languages and his articles feature regularly in major Christian publications. The Next Wave International websites attract thousands of visitors from around the world every month.

Originally from Australia, Mal is known in many nations as a pioneer leader and for his unique ability to communicate Christian truth in a thought-provoking, insightful, and often humorous way that relates to secular and Christian audiences alike.

Mal was raised in a Christian home, and studied architecture in his home city of Melbourne before feeling a call to full-time ministry in the early 1980s. Throughout the eighties and early nineties, he was the key pioneer of *Youth Alive Australia* and its first National Director. This exciting movement grew from just 300 young people to over 60,000 in 10 years, as the Spirit of God moved among that nation's youth and churches. It continues to grow and its model is now influencing many nations for Jesus.

About the Author

Mal also pioneered a church in one of his country's leading New Age and occult areas.

Today, as well as heading up the mission to Europe and working in the media, Mal travels the world extensively, teaching and preaching at leadership conferences and events. He has been married to Davina for more than twenty years and they have three children.

Information on Mal's personal appearances, plus photos, articles, audio files and books can be found at: www.malfletcher.com.

If you've enjoyed reading this book, check out these other great resources from Mal Fletcher at:

www.malfletcher.com

- Mal's *Daily Recharge* – an inspiring daily devotional for every day of the year.
- *Social Comment* – short and concise, each social comment follows a hot issue or event confronting society today.
- *Life & Leadership* articles – thought-provoking articles providing helpful perspectives on the challenges of twenty-first-century life.
- Mal's *Recommended Reading List* – including a new 'Book of the Month' each month.
- *EDGES™ with Mal Fletcher* programmes – watch full half-hour episodes from the popular TV series online (programmes also available on DVD).
- *Audio Messages* – listen to many of Mal's inspiring messages recorded at events from around the world (download as MP3 or stream online).
- *GodSpots* – 30-second audio files, presenting positive responses to life problems and questions.
- *TimeOut* clips – short TV spots that look at everyday life from a hope-filled Christian perspective.
- *News* – about the work of Next Wave International, in Europe and beyond.
- Sign up for *E-News* – keep in touch with the work of Mal and Next Wave International, in Europe and around the world.
- *Webshop* – containing books, eBooks, DVDs and CDs.

**You Can Help Mal Fletcher and His Team
Make a Permanent Impact on Europe!**

According to respected Christian leaders like C. Peter Wagner, Western Europe now represents perhaps the darkest region on earth, in spiritual terms.

*Every day, 30,000 people come to Christ in Latin America.
Every day, 25,000 come to Christ in China.
Every day, 15,000 come to Christ in Africa.
Every day, up to 7,000 people leave the church in Europe!*

Mal Fletcher and Next Wave International™ are helping to reshape Europe's spiritual future!

Yes, I want to help Mal and his international team by investing in this rapidly growing mission across Europe.

GIVE ONLINE. IT'S SECURE, FAST & EASY
www.malfletcher.com
(Use a credit card, direct transfer or Pay Pal account)

<u>OR</u> FILL OUT THE FORM BELOW

Name: _____

Address: _____

Email: _____ Phone: _____

Please debit my:
☐ Visa ☐ Master Card

Card No.: ☐☐☐☐ – ☐☐☐☐ – ☐☐☐☐ – ☐☐☐☐

Name on Card: _____

Expiry Date: _____/_____ Signature: _____

Amount (please include your currency): _____

This is a: ☐ Monthly Pledge ☐ One-Time Gift

Mail/fax to:
EUROPE/BRITAIN/USA/CANADA/REST OF WORLD
(except *below):
Next Wave International, 155 Regents Park Road, London,
NW1 8BB, United Kingdom

*AUSTRALIA / NEW ZEALAND / ASIA:
Next Wave International, PO Box 93, O'Halloran Hill,
South Australia, 5158, Australia
Fax: +61 8 8322 8101